BOOKS BY
DAVID HOWARTH

Trafalgar: The Nelson Touch   1969

Waterloo: Day of Battle   1968

Panama   1966

The Desert King   1964

My Land and My People (EDITOR)   1962

The Shadow of the Dam   1961

D Day   1959

The Sledge Patrol   1957

We Die Alone   1955

Thieves' Hole   1954

Across to Norway   1952

WATERLOO: DAY OF BATTLE

WATERLOO

DAY OF BATTLE

DAVID HOWARTH

GALAHAD BOOKS · NEW YORK CITY

Published in Great Britain under the title
A Near Run Thing: The Day of Waterloo
Copyright © 1968 by David Howarth
All rights reserved
Library of Congress Catalog Card Number: 74-77012
ISBN 0-88365-273-0
Manufactured in the United States of America
Published by arrangement with Atheneum

INTRODUCTION

'After the publication of so many accounts of the battle of the 18th of June, it may fairly be asked on what grounds I expect to awaken fresh interest in a subject so long before the public.' This was written by Sergeant-Major Edward Cotton in the preface of his book about Waterloo, which was published over a hundred years ago. Since then, a great many more accounts have been written, and now the question may even more fairly be asked. So I must answer it.

Waterloo was a most ferocious battle, an experience both harrowing and thrilling for the men who survived it: the total defeat of an empire, inflicted in a single Sunday afternoon on a field of battle only two miles long and two-thirds of a mile across. It was also a controversial battle. After the fighting was over, Napoleon blamed his marshals for the disaster, Prussians and British bickered over their shares of the victory, and officers of rival regiments argued about each other's claims of glory. I think too much has been written about the arguments, and too little about the experience.

The earliest accounts of the battle, in prose and verse, were written in a heroic style that many people even then, including the Duke of Wellington, knew was far from reality. Later, there were technical accounts, written by officers who were there, and read, one can only suppose, by officers who were not. Then, after the last survivors were dead, the controversy became the main topic, and many books, especially since the turn of the century, have analysed the orders given by Wellington and Napoleon, and the marshals' actions and the movements of regiments, in the smallest detail.

That kind of critical analysis is the essence of military history, and it has an intellectual interest of its own. But it is not the essence of a battle: it does not describe a human experience. Historians can see a battle calmly as a whole, but no soldier in battle sees anything of the sort. He is half-blinded by gunsmoke, half-deafened by noise, and either half-paralysed by fright or driven to a kind of madness by exaltation and the hope of glory. The more thoroughly you analyse a battle, in the light of after-knowledge, the harder it becomes to remember what it felt like to the people who were in it.

And criticism, I think, can go too far. Every high commander at Waterloo, except perhaps Marshal Blücher, has been accused of blunders by armchair critics: not only Napoleon and his marshals, who lost, but Wellington and some of his generals, who won. It seems to me absurd that anyone nowadays, however learned he may be, can persuade himself he would have known better than they did at the time. All commanders make their decisions on the experience and information they possess, and it can only be legitimate now to say that they made mistakes if their own colleagues said so there and then, like the Prince of Orange's colleagues, or if they said so themselves, like Lord Uxbridge. I am only surprised that anyone in the thick of a battle like Waterloo can make any wise decisions at all. Ney's judgement, for example, may have been less than perfect; but he had five horses shot under him during the afternoon.

However, the Napoleonic Wars were the first in which it is still possible to see a battle from the soldier's ground-level, smoke-shrouded point of view, because they were the first in which enough of the soldiers were literate. Many junior officers, sergeants and even privates wrote reminiscences or letters after Waterloo, some very soon after, to reassure their families, and some many years after, to occupy their old age. These soldiers' stories have nothing to say about strategy and not very much about tactics, and so they are only sparsely used, on the whole, in the critical histories. But some of them give very clear impressions of the tiny part of a battle which is all that a soldier sees.

In this book, I have tried to go back to the beginning, as it were, to describe the battle as it appeared, on the day it was fought, to the men who fought in it. The book only tells the soldiers' story, without any scholarly afterthoughts: what they saw and heard and felt, the little that they knew, the trivialities they remembered afterwards, and their elementary idea of what it was all about. I have not quoted directly very much of what they wrote, because masses of quotations are tedious to read, and because their style seems quaint, which is only a distraction. They were not quaint at all. Behind their stilted prose, and underneath their peacock uniforms, they were much the same kind of people as their descendants are today. One can still understand their feelings. Among all the accounts of the vast historic drama, my favourite was given by a very small British soldier on the morning after. 'I'll be hanged if I know anything about the matter,' was all he could find to say, 'for I was all day trodden in the mud and ridden over by every scoundrel who had a horse.'

It is not my business to praise or blame them: I have tried to see them as they saw themselves. But also, I have tried to use my own understanding of people, such as it is, to discover *why* they acted as they did. Here and there, this has led me beyond the limits I meant to set myself: for example, I have put in some speculations about Napoleon's health. Napoleon did make mistakes, he was not himself: his generals knew he was making them, and said so, and wondered what was wrong with him. At that time, they could not guess, but now one can. The questions they asked themselves were part of the experience of the day, and it would have been foolish, I think, to report the questions without the most probable answers.

This is not a work of scholarship, so I have not dignified it with a list of sources. It is based on eighteen principal eye-witness accounts, about the same number of biographies and memoirs, and a large number of letters which added isolated details. All of them can be found in libraries either in London, Paris or Brussels. For the general events of the battle, I mostly relied on Captain Siborne's history, published in 1844 (which I suppose is the most detailed, authoritative and boring account of a battle ever written), and from the French side that of Henry Houssaye, published in 1898. I chose the eye-witnesses not only for the merit of what they wrote, but also for their differences, so that their individual stories could be put together to make a continuous narrative of the day. I am only sorry a disproportionate number of them are British: the British wrote much more about the battle than the French or anyone else, no doubt because they thought they had more to be proud of.

There is a moral in the story, for anyone who cares to look for it. Of course, what a general does in a battle is more important than what a soldier does, or what he feels or thinks; but the deeds and thoughts of soldiers have a special interest, because they sometimes illuminate the mystery of military life. The mystery is this: what makes a man, who joins an army and puts on a more or less exotic kind of dress, behave on the word of command entirely unlike himself, but like a ferocious animal? This is a question of more than historical interest, because the same thing still has to happen in any successful army when it goes to war.

Waterloo was an extreme case of this strange behaviour. The combatants on both sides were ordinary men with ordinary, homely faults and virtues. French and British soldiers admired each other. Yet the battle they fought was not the impersonal, scientific kind of battle that armies fight nowadays. They hacked and slashed at each other with sabres, lances and bayonets, shot each other point-blank with muskets and pistols, and triumphantly mowed each other down with grape-shot from cannon at thirty paces, until one in four of them was lying dead or wounded and the field was encumbered with the heaps of corpses. Why did they do it? Why do men ever do it—and women never? Why, on the other hand, did 10,000 men of Wellington's army run away? And why did the French, who had been attacking all the afternoon, suddenly change in the course of ten minutes from an army to a rabble?

In the soldiers' tales of Waterloo there are glimpses of the answers of these questions. Most of the men who wrote them down were lacking in introspection, and less critical of authority and the established order than anyone is today. So they reveal unconsciously the muddled hopes that took them there, the fear that trapped them and the pride that blinded them.

But with or without a moral, I hope it still makes a good story, which is all I meant it to be.

CONTENTS

MAPS

DAWN

The men — Their hopes and fears
Ligny and Quatre Bras

DAWN

It had rained all night. At dawn, in the fields of rye along the southern edge of the forest of Soignes, you could hear a murmur like the sea on a distant shore. This was the blended voices of 67,000 men, grumbling, yawning, shivering, stretching cramped limbs, joking as people do when they share discomfort, and arguing about what would happen next: not about what Napoleon would do or what the Duke would do, but about more pressing problems: where to find something dry to light a fire, where to look for the wagons with the gin rations, and whether there was anything for breakfast. It was the dawn of Sunday, 18 June 1815.

Of all those thousands of men, most were entirely forgotten long ago. But some wrote down what happened to them that day or, if they could not write, told the story to someone who could: and those can still be observed as they crouched in the dripping corn that miserable morning. There, for example, within a few hundred yards of each other, although they had never heard of each other and never met, were William Leeke, who was only seventeen; Cavalié Mercer, an artist and captain of artillery; Tom Morris, an argumentative Cockney sergeant; William Wheeler and William Lawrence, two old soldiers who knew all the tricks of the trade; John Kincaid, who was a regular captain but looked on the bloodiest battles with a humorous sporting eye; and Rees Howell Gronow, an old Etonian soon to be celebrated as a dandy and raconteur.

*   *   *

As the daylight grew, it showed to each man first his own companions, muddy and unshaven; and then his own regiment's bivouac, the piled muskets, the officers' horses tethered to bayonets driven

into the ground, the rows of men still lying with their heads on their knapsacks and a sodden blanket over each of them. Then it showed other regiments: cavalry, the hundreds of horses picketed line after line, and artillery, cannon and limbers and ammunition wagons, some that had been there at dusk the evening before, and some that had come in the night. And finally, as the sky lightened and men began to succeed in their search for sticks and straw, columns of smoke rose far and near among the woods and rolling fields, and showed that scores of other regiments, most of the Duke of Wellington's army, must be there.

Not one of those seven men, and very few of the 67,000, knew what was happening. They knew the French were coming and Napoleon himself was leading them, and that was all they really wanted to know: nobody paid you to worry in the army. The Duke was in command, they were perfectly sure he knew what he was doing, and sooner or later their own officers would tell them what to do. It might be retreat, or it might be a battle. And if it was a battle, the veterans boasted, the Duke was their man: under the

Duke, old Nosey, they had always beaten the French and they would do it again, and no matter if every one of the Frenchmen was a Napoleon.

But although they did not know what was happening, most of them had a good idea of what they were there for. Perhaps they saw things in terms that were rather too simple, but to the British at least in Wellington's army it all seemed plain. For eighteen years, Napoleon and his armies had overrun and terrorized more and more of Europe. Most of that time, the families of the British soldiers had lived in fear of invasion, and the younger soldiers themselves had been brought up with Napoleon as a familiar bogy. Then at last he had overreached himself and been beaten—and Wellington and his British troops, fighting through the Spanish peninsula, had been able to claim a good share of the credit for his downfall. In April 1814, only just over a year before, Napoleon had been sent into exile on the island of Elba. A glorious wave of relief had swept over England, and Wellington's well-tried army had been disbanded, or scattered to America, Ireland and the East. And then, in March, Napoleon had escaped, landed in France, marched on Paris and been received by the French again with acclamation. There was only one thing to do—to beat him again. Europe was united against him. Russian, German, Austrian, Prussian, British, Dutch and Belgian armies—all were on the move. But he had re-formed his army incredibly quickly, and assembled it on the north-east frontier of France. The only armies which could be brought within striking distance were the Prussians under Marshal Blücher, who were in the south of Belgium, and Wellington's mixed command, which was in the north. So it was up to them.

The British soldiers did not hate the French: on the contrary, they admired their martial skill, and grudgingly admired Napoleon's most of all. Wellington himself had written: 'France has no enemies, as

far as I know. I am sure that she does not deserve to have any. We are the enemies of one man only, and of his partisans.' He was to seem less logical that very afternoon when an artillery officer had a clear view of Napoleon and asked if he should fire. 'Certainly not, I will not allow it,' the Duke replied. 'It is not the business of commanders to fire upon each other.'

So the British, casually waiting in bored discomfort for what the day might bring, had a clearer conception of what they were doing than many soldiers since. Napoleon had to be stopped, and that was that. But only one-third of Wellington's army was British. The rest were Dutch, Belgians and Germans, some veteran exiles and some young conscripts. For them the issue was not so simple. The British had never been invaded by the French, but all the others had. The Belgians in particular had suffered so many foreign dominations and political changes that their loyalties were thoroughly muddled. After being governed from Spain and then from Austria, they had been made a province of France by Napoleon; and when Napoleon fell, their country had been awarded by the victorious powers, without any regard for their own wishes, to the newly created King of Holland. Many of Wellington's Belgian troops had fought for Napoleon, instead of against him, not many years before. Some of his Belgian officers knew their old regiments and comrades in arms were lined up on the other side. Moreover, they were preparing to fight in their own country, and they and their families would have to live with whichever army won. So all they could be expected to want was to be on the winning side.

Nor did their own commander add to their confidence. He was the Prince of Orange, the son of the new King of Holland. The Duke had had to accept the Prince in this high position—second only to himself in seniority—because the army was assembled in what had now become Dutch territory. But it was a rather ludicrous appointment, because the Prince was only twenty-two years old. He was a product of the hectic changes of Europe in that period. His archaic hereditary title meant very little: the Principality of Orange, which was near Avignon in the south of France, had ceased to exist 150 years before. He had been born in Holland, but had lived in exile, in London and Berlin, since he was three. He was at Oxford as an undergraduate, and his only military service had been as an aide-de-camp to the Duke in Spain. Now, although he was hardly more than

a boy, he suddenly and unexpectedly found himself crown prince
of a country he did not know, and general in command of some
40,000 men. British officers thought him an amiable and brave but
not very clever young fellow, and they hoped he would not try to
give too many orders.

It was hardly surprising that Wellington mistrusted his Belgian
troops and, for similar reasons, his Dutch and most of his Germans.
Some of the British soldiers despised them. Some, more sympathetic
and understanding, were sorry for them. But nobody was happy to
have them as allies and neighbours in the battle line. 'All in all,' one
Scottish officer wrote afterwards, 'we were a very bad army'—and
that was the general opinion. 'An infamous army' was the phrase
that Wellington chose to use.

*   *   *

William Leeke, seventeen years old, understood even less than most
men what was happening, although he was an officer: an ensign in
the 52nd Foot. He knew he was in Belgium, but that was all. He had
shared his cloak and a bundle of straw all night in a muddy field with
another officer not much older than himself. The cloak was too
small to cover them both, so they both got very wet. A few horses
had broken loose and galloped about all night like a charge of
cavalry, and the two young men, for fear of being trampled on,
often jumped up to scare the animals away. Whenever Leeke dozed,
he dreamed that he was charging into battle, and when he lay awake
he thought of home. Home was quite a recent recollection. He had
been in the army just over a month, and it was only six weeks since
his mother had hugged him and kissed him good-bye, and begged
him at the last moment not to choose such a dangerous profession.

Leeke was the younger son of a country squire in Hampshire. His
father had meant him for the Church, but when he left school at
sixteen he rebelled against being a parson, and thought of the Law
instead. At a ball, however, he met a young officer who had just
come back from Spain. He listened entranced to his stories of active
service under Wellington, and decided that very night to join the
army. Since his father was a gentleman, and also could afford to buy
him a commission, there was never any thought of joining in the
ranks. His family wrote to relatives who had influence, and he was

offered a choice of America in an infantry regiment or India with the cavalry. The American revolution seemed to him to be coming to an end, so he preferred the cavalry and India. But on one day in March, everything changed. He read in the paper that peace had been ratified in America, and finally made up his mind for a life in India—and then in a later edition of the same paper he saw the news that Napoleon had escaped from Elba. So it was not too late to share the excitement and glory of the Napoleonic war, which everyone had thought was over. He wrote at once to a cousin in the 52nd Foot, which he had heard was going to Belgium. He was accepted, and set off for Belgium alone to catch up with the regiment—a journey in which everything was new and exciting, and almost everything delightful. In London, escorted by a kindly colonel of the Guards, he bought the elaborate, romantic and splendid outfit of an infantry officer: the uniforms, boat-cloak, sword and pistols, the valise, the camp bed and blankets, and the canteen of plates, knives and forks, unbreakable wineglasses, kettle and soup tureen, and two three-pint bottles which he wisely had filled with the best brandy, although he did not like it. In Dover, he daringly entered a billiards saloon, where he won some money from some other officers, and having been well brought up contrived to lose it all on a final game. Crossing the Channel, he was so sick he wished the ship would sink, but in Ostend he was revived by seeing some men unloading cannon balls, pitching them up from the hold like bricklayers throwing bricks; and he bought a baggage horse to carry his purchases. On a canal boat going to Ghent, he met a friendly major-general, who produced two ginger biscuits from a paper bag and gave him one of them. After school and home, it was all like a boyish dream.

There must have been some charm in William Leeke's simplicity. He was ignorant and innocent, and the 52nd, which he was joining, was a proud and distinguished regiment of veterans from the Peninsular War. Yet everyone was kind to him. His brother officers (as he learned to call them) laughed at him when he spoke of the side of the company instead of the flank, and of being behind it instead of being in the rear. They told him that if he was lucky he would soon be a field officer—which meant, he discovered, not a general or a marshal but an officer dead and buried beneath the sod. But it was all done with good humour. When the colonel told him he ought to buy a riding horse (most infantry officers were mounted), he said he had meant to try to do without one until after the first action, when no doubt many officers would be killed and horses would be going cheap. The colonel only smiled, but Leeke found a horse and bought it, a big black one with a long tail. At least he was a competent horseman and could hold his own in the officers' steeplechases: and that was really all that was expected of a new recruit. Before the month was out, he had started to look on the officers' mess as a new family circle, to which he happily gave his pride and loyalty. He was already under the spell of army life.

Then, one morning, an aide-de-camp came cantering through the village they were quartered in, the bugles sounded the assembly, the band struck up and the regiment marched to war: Ensign Leeke riding ahead of his men, each of whom, on foot, was carrying a knapsack with all his possessions, a musket and bayonet and 120 rounds of ball cartridge. For two days they marched and countermarched, a confusing pattern across the Belgian countryside. Once, when they halted to cook, some wagons of wounded passed them. Often they passed soldiers, and drummer boys and women, who had fallen out exhausted from the march of other regiments. It was clear that all the army was on the move. During the 17th, they heard artillery, and that evening they saw some French troops in the

From a Rowlandson etching of the life of an ensign in Wellington's army

distance, and the order was given to load. But night was falling, the alert subsided, and the order came to bivouac where they were.

Apart from the Channel crossing, that wet night out in the corn-field was the only unpleasant thing that had happened to William Leeke. Even that, he was sharing with his friends. At dawn, when he was wet and shivering, he saw a fire a little distance off, with a few officers standing round it. He wandered towards it. It belonged to another regiment, but they let him warm himself. There was a plank on the ground beside it, about his own length, and he lay down on it: and there he fell fast asleep, totally unprepared for what the day would bring.

*　　　*　　　*

Two miles north of the 52nd's bivouac, there were two more men called William: Sergeants William Lawrence and William Wheeler. Leeke only knew very vaguely where he was, but both the sergeants knew exactly. The day before, they had both been marching on a main road with their regiments, although in opposite directions, and night overtook them both at a village with the odd and unexpected name of Waterloo. When they halted, all the cottages were already full of officers. Lawrence's regiment packed itself in barns and cowsheds. Wheeler's had to use an open field.

Billeted on the peasants

William Lawrence's home was not far from William Leeke's: it was in the village of Bryant's Piddle in Dorset. His entry into the army, like Leeke's, was perfectly typical of the times, although it was totally different. His father was neither a gentleman nor a squire; he had been a farmer in a small way, but he had seven children, which so reduced him in circumstances that he had to give up his farm and work as a labourer. When William was a small boy, he earned 2d. a day as a bird scarer: then he advanced to 6d. a day as a plough-boy. When he was fourteen, his father borrowed £20 to buy him an apprenticeship, and bound him for seven years to a builder, who agreed to feed and house and clothe him, but not to pay him any wages. As it turned out, however, the builder also beat him with a horse whip, and before he was fifteen, he stole 7s. and a piece of bacon and ran away, to wander round Dorset under the threat of gaol.

The army was a natural refuge for a friendless, destitute, fugitive little boy. It was always in need of recruits, and in every town it had sergeants who had authority to pay a handsome sum to any likely boy, and to anyone who brought him to the recruiting station. It could pay off fines and debts, and bully cruel masters and unsympathetic magistrates: 'and when a miscreant boy had taken the oath and put on a uniform, the civil authorities were usually glad to wash their hands of him, believing with some reason that whoever else had failed, the army would make a man of him. In Dorchester, William Lawrence volunteered for the artillery, but his father found out and sent him back to his master. Before he reached the master's house he ran away again, and fell in with a soldier on leave who took him to Bridport and Taunton, hawking him round the sergeants of different regiments to find which would pay the most for him. He finished up in the 40th Regiment Foot, and after a few weeks' drill he was shipped to Rio de Janeiro. In the eight years since then, he had fought through South America, Portugal and Spain, had camped on the banks of the Mississippi, had been wounded many times, and had sometimes regretted his escapade and wished he was laying bricks. He had never been back to England.

After all those years, there was nothing whatever that Lawrence needed to learn about the army: not only how to fight and live to fight again, but also how to avoid the punishments of four or five hundred lashes with the cat, which put evil-doers to hospital for weeks if they did not kill them, and how to make the best of life campaigning in a foreign country. The army only provided enough to keep its men alive and active—bread, gin and lumps of beef which they had to cook for themselves whenever they were moving—and the commissariat wagons which carried these meagre supplies were sometimes left behind or lost. The Duke, on the other hand, would not tolerate looting, and offered no reprieve to serious offenders who were sentenced to be shot. But there were all degrees of looting. Some things, including the property of enemy soldiers, were legitimate spoils of war, and it was a poor soldier who never happened to find a few comforts—a stray chicken, a pig, or a barrel of wine or beer.

All this was perfectly understood, by officers and men alike; and Wellington's officers and men, though they grumbled at his strictness, also agreed on the whole that his policy was best. Life was more comfortable in the end if they restrained themselves. They were nearly always in country that remembered a French occupation, and the people were often so astonished to find they were not being outrageously robbed that they welcomed the British soldiers like sons and brothers. And this welcome, in turn, domesticated the toughest of soldiers, and caused them to play with the children, give

help to the housewives and farmers, and woo the daughters with almost the same decorum that they would have shown at home.

For these reasons, Sergeant Lawrence and Sergeant Wheeler, by their own standards, had been living in luxury in Belgium: so had the whole of the army. Wheeler, for the past two months, had been billeted with a tobacconist's family in the village of Grammont. He drew his army rations every day, and kept the gin and gave the food to the mistress of the house. She cooked the beef if it was good, and if it was not she gave it, with the bread, to local beggars: and she fed her lodgers three excellent meals a day. Once, when the regiment went away for a week, it was welcomed back to Grammont with church bells and feasting and a public holiday, and Wheeler never heard of any disagreement between the army and the Belgian people —except when some officers out on a spree in Brussels lassoed the celebrated statue Mannekin Pis and pulled him headfirst into the basin of water beneath him. Romances flowered freely, but Wheeler wrote home that he did not mean to get entangled. 'It might be all very fine in its way, and no doubt there are many sweets in having a pretty lovely young woman for a comrade, but then, I know from observation that there is an infinite number of bitters attending it, a soldier should always be able to say, when his cap is on his family is covered, then he is free as air.'

After this halcyon life, the two days' march to the muddy field at the village of Waterloo needed all of Wheeler's soldierly philosophy: but this, he knew, was what they had come for. The march was enlivened by a single bit of luck. Marching through a village, they met a regiment of Belgian cavalry riding hell for leather in the opposite direction. They assumed they were changing position, and halted to let them pass; but afterwards they heard they were running away from battle. That gave an added zest to what happened. A Belgian officer fell off his horse and dropped his purse, and Wheeler and his companions snatched it up. That night, in Waterloo, they found a man who was selling brandy and gin, and used their windfall to buy themselves plenty of both. So they sat on their knapsacks all night, with the water running in streams from the cuffs of their jackets, and the bottles passing round. As one of them said, they were wet and comfortable.

Sergeant Lawrence's regiment, the day before, had marched through the middle of Brussels. The people of the city came out in the streets to give them refreshments, and to tell them with ghoulish sympathy that Napoelon was coming and they would all be slaughtered like bullocks. The old hands from the Peninsula laughed and said they were used to that. Some of Lawrence's young recruits, he noticed, were very downcast and frightened, but in his experience it was often the most timid who, if it came to a battle, rushed forward and got killed first through their own confusion of mind.

That night, in his cowshed close to the main road, Lawrence listened to the sounds of men and carts and horses continually passing northwards up the road to Brussels. Some of these were the local peasantry, abandoning their farms and cottages and seeking refuge in the forest of Soignes. Some, an unusually large and ominous number, were deserters. The rest were camp followers: the sutlers, who were travelling merchants, the officers' servants taking their baggage and baggage horses out of harm's way, the commissary men, the supernumeraries like regimental tailors and blacksmiths, and the army's wives and children—and also, though people only mentioned them obliquely, the ladies of easier virtue. The endless traffic northwards suggested to everyone who heard it that something important was happening, or was about to happen, in the south.

*   *   *

Cavalié Mercer, the captain of artillery, had a somewhat better idea of what was happening than most of the men who were waiting in that dawn—not because anyone had told him, but because he had been in action, in a fighting retreat, the whole of the day before. Dawn found him sitting under an umbrella with his second-in-command in the hedge of an orchard, smoking a cigar. Before him under the apple trees was the pride of his life: his troop of five nine-pounder guns and one heavy howitzer, six officers, 184 well-trained and cheerful men, and 220 superb horses. 'Mein Gott,' old Marshal Blücher, commander of the allied Prussian army, had cried when he inspected them a week or two before, 'mein Gott, dere is not von orse in dies batterie vich is not goot for Veldt Marshal.'

 ˙ Mercer was thirty-two, the son of a general: all his family were in the army or the navy. He had passed through the Military Academy at Woolwich and been commissioned when he was sixteen, and had lived on active service most of his adult life. Training, from the

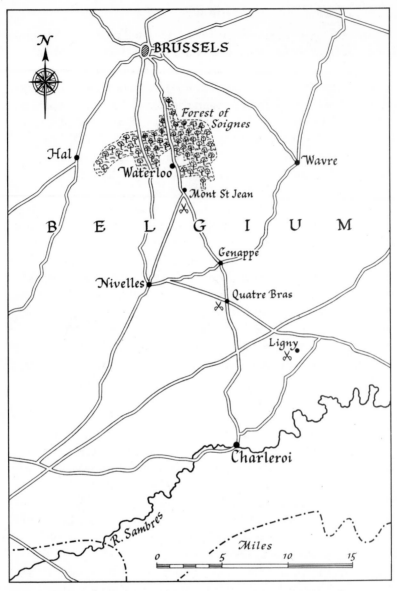

Quatre Bras and Ligny

cradle up, had made him a thoroughly professional officer: it did not prevent him being an amateur artist with an eye for the picturesque, or seeing the comic and ludicrous aspects of army life. Indeed, he was a notably gentle, humane and civilized man. What he had enjoyed most, in the weeks of waiting, was not the balls and dinner parties,

Captain Cavalié Mercer

but walking or riding alone in the wild, neglected park of a château near his billet and talking to its owner, a highly eccentric Belgian nobleman who always wore Turkish costume. He liked quiet, and rural peace and beauty, more than the panoply and clamour of the army. The day before had been exciting, dangerous and bloody, but the only thing he recalled with horror was seeing some soldiers chasing a pig and bringing it down with axes, musket butts and bayonets. He never questioned the paradox of war: he would do his utmost to kill an active enemy soldier, and do his utmost to help a wounded one.

When Mercer had received the order to move from his billets, two days before, early in the morning of Friday the 16th, he had set off to march his troop through the winding Belgian lanes, steering more by instinct and common sense than by any rational method, and picking up scraps of information from other commanding officers as lost as he was. About midday, he was puzzled to see one of the Duke's aides-de-camp posting along on a weary sweating horse, but apparently dressed for a ball in white pantaloons and an embroidered suit. During the afternoon, he was guided by the sound of gunfire, and then by a straggling procession of wounded men coming down the lanes towards him: many, he noticed with foreboding, were escorted by six, eight or even ten unwounded comrades who pretended to be looking after them. These groups—they were Belgians or Germans—told him the day was lost and the British routed. But the only British soldier among them, a private of the Gordon Highlanders with a musket-ball lodged in his knee, said that was a damned lie. 'They war fechtin' yet an I laft 'em, but it's a bludy business.' Mercer waited while his battery doctor seated the Scotsman on the parapet of a bridge and gouged out the musket-ball.

Then he pressed eagerly on, and at dusk, twenty miles south of Brussels, he approached the crossroads called Quatre Bras. Here, shot and shell were flying overhead, bugles and musketry were heard in the neighbouring woods, and in the half light his horses stumbled over dead men lying in the road. But the noise was slackening: he was just too late to join the battle that had been raging there all day.

The troop made a bivouac that night in a hilly field which overlooked the crossroads, and Mercer slept in peace on the muddy ground: for armies in those days seldom moved or fought in the dark. It was not until next morning that he found a staff officer who could give him any news. Even then, it was sketchy, but so far as it went it was correct. The battle round the crossroads—the battle of Quatre Bras—had been fought by a few haphazard units of Wellington's army, any who chanced to be there, a mixture of British, Belgian and German troops. The result had been inconclusive, but at least they had held their own. Fresh troops had been arriving all the time, and everyone was confident that when the battle started again in the morning, they would be led to the attack and would beat whatever Napoleon could send against them.

But during the day, news had been brought of a bigger battle five miles to the south-east, at the village of Ligny. There, the Prussian army under Blücher, a force that was stronger and larger than Wellington's, had met the right wing of Napoleon's army and had been defeated and forced to retire towards the north: and Wellington had had to order his army to retire in consequence. It was a disappointment to men who thought they had done very well and had not had a chance, so far, to show they could do even better. The officer who gave the gloomy news to Mercer informed him also that he was to have the honour of forming the rearguard of artillery to cover the infantry in the retreat.

The retreat began early in the morning, the infantry regiments marching away up the road to Waterloo and Brussels, and being replaced as they went by others drawn in from the flanks, in order to hide the movement from the French. But the French did nothing. All the morning, Mercer sat on his hill watching skirmishers taking pot-shots at each other among the hedges down below him, and he never saw a target worthy of his guns. The quiet was mystifying: the British at that moment of retreat were vulnerable, and Napoleon, for all his fearsome reputation, was missing an opportunity. But by

Lord Uxbridge

midday the army had gone: Mercer's battery was alone, with not
a living man in sight except a few pickets of cavalry. The smoke of
the French camp fires rose calmly beyond the trees. As he watched,

a horseman came cantering up to join him, followed by an aide-de-camp: Lord Uxbridge, commander of the British cavalry. His Lordship dismounted, and they sat on the ground together. 'It will not be long now before they are on us,' said the aide-de-camp, 'for they always dine before they move, and those smokes seem to indicate that they are cooking now.' And soon a column of French cavalry came into view. Lord Uxbridge rode away, and Mercer, left all alone, limbered up and galloped back to join the cavalry.

The afternoon opened with heavy thunderclouds overhead, inky black, casting a deep obscurity over the British position, while the distant hills where the French had bivouacked still remained in sunshine; and on to this stage, which seemed to be illuminated for a melodramatic entrance, a single horseman rode, followed at an interval by others, and stood for a moment silhouetted against the sunlit distances on the hill that Mercer had left. It was the best-known figure in Europe, and Mercer knew it at once: the Emperor Napoleon. Squadrons of French chasseurs then came over the brow of the hill behind him, and Lord Uxbridge shouted 'Fire! Fire!' Mercer discharged all his guns at the group and limbered up and galloped off again, while a French battery opened fire on him.

After that, the retreat was a leap-frog of Mercer's troop and Uxbridge's cavalry, elements of the Life Guards and the Blues—an affair of hurried artillery duels and exhilarating gallops back to safety, in which Lord Uxbridge, as excited as a boy, kept charging about under fire hallooing on his men and Mercer's like a young lieutenant. ('The prettiest Field Day of Cavalry and Horse Artillery that I ever witnessed,' he wrote afterwards.) The clouds burst, rain came down like a water-spout, flashes of lightning and peals of thunder almost drowned the gunfire. Sometimes the troop was on the heels of the allied infantry: often it was close enough to the French pursuit to hear their mocking shouts of laughter. At last Mercer came to a sand pit on rising ground that seemed to be deserted, and he turned once more to fire: and while his first shot was echoing, he was startled by a heavy cannonade from a hedge behind him. It was the main body of the army: the retreat, for the moment, was over, and the infantry was intact.

He was also a little startled, about the same time, by an elderly man in a shabby old drab greatcoat and a rusty round hat, who came rambling among the guns and engaged him in conversation about

the events of the day. Mercer took him for a sightseer from Brussels
—there were said to be several about—and he thought his questions
were impertinent, so he gave him short answers: and he was abashed
when he heard soon after that this was General Sir Thomas Picton,
a revered and celebrated figure in the army, who had arrived from
England to command an infantry division and had lost his uniform.
The general's shambling gait had a possible explanation that Mercer
never heard of: he had been wounded in the hip at Quatre Bras, and
for fear of being invalided out he had not told anyone about it except
his valet.

The orchard where Mercer spent the night was close to the sand
pit, on the other side of the main road. It belonged to a farm called
La Haye Sainte, but by the time his day's work was done, the farm
buildings were already crammed with officers and men: so after his
hectic day, he spent the night in as much discomfort as anyone. His
men had brought three days' rations with them ready-cooked, and
hay for the horses. That had been his own order. But he and his six
officers had not been so provident. They had had nothing to eat for
the past two days, except one left-over piece of pie which they carefully divided into seven equal fragments. At dawn, a German soldier
who had lost his regiment pushed through the hedge of the orchard
and asked if he could warm himself at Mercer's fire: and having done
that, and smoked a pipe, he pulled out a half-starved chicken from
his haversack and offered it to Mercer with his thanks. The officers
hastily put it on to boil, but they were too hungry to wait, and
before it was half-cooked they pulled it to pieces and ate it. Mercer
got a leg.

Just after dawn, a bombardier he had sent up the Brussels road the
night before for ammunition came back and reported the road was
in chaos. Many of the wagons which Sergeant Lawrence had heard
as they passed through Waterloo had stuck or overturned in the mud
and been plundered. He himself had happened, he said, to find some
beef, biscuits, oatmeal and rum which did not seem to have an
owner. There was enough rum for the whole of the troop, and they
made the oatmeal into what the army called stirabout: and Mercer,
with his most important problem solved, mounted his horse and
went to reconnoitre.

The gentle ridge he had seen deserted the night before was now
covered with troops, cleaning their arms, cooking, or sitting round

The village of Waterloo; Wellington's headquarters were on the left

their camp fires smoking. Officers were strolling about or standing in groups conversing. To the south, across a shallow valley, he could see the French on a parallel ridge. They seemed to be equally quiet and unconcerned: he supposed they were also equally cold and wet. All the officers he met, seeing him mounted and knowing perhaps that he had been in action, asked him for news. All of them were speculating. Some thought the French would not dare to attack, some that they would do so very soon; some thought the Duke would wait for it, and others, most of them, expected the retreat to continue, at least as far as the approach to Brussels. But in the meantime, until they heard the Duke's decision, there was nothing to be done. Mercer rode back to the orchard, left his horse and strolled into the garden of the farm: he always went to look at gardens when he could. There he found some Guardsmen digging potatoes. That seemed to him a useful occupation, and he called a few of his men to help, and began to dig.

*   *   *

Two other men who were in the retreat shared much the same experience as Mercer, but regarded it with very different eyes. These were Tom Morris, the Cockney sergeant, and John Kincaid, a Scottish captain in the Rifle Brigade. Morris, whose infantry regiment was one of the last to march, saw more than most infantrymen of Lord Uxbridge's rearguard action, because he stopped to take some gravel out of his boots. He had also stopped, a little earlier on the way, to acquire a good supply of what he called malt liquor. It was in a gentleman's cellar, and perhaps he could not give it a more specific name, because he and his companions stove in all the casks in the cellar and waded knee-deep in the mixture to fill their canteens. Kincaid, on the other hand, did not see any fighting that day, because he simply carried out his orders and took his company back to a place of safety.

Each of these men was a type well known in British armies: better known in armies than in civilian life because armies bring out their innate characters. Morris was the man who always thought he knew best, the eternal grouser, the ranker who really ought to have been in command. As a sergeant, he criticized Wellington's conduct of Quatre Bras. And his own captain, he said, had been in the army for upward of thirty years and never in action before, so that he lost his head under fire and would have got the whole company killed if other officers had not told him what to do. He was the kind of man who cannot bear to hear another man praised, and cannot bear to admit himself mistaken.

Kincaid, on the other hand, was a brave man who could never have brought himself to say so. He readily admired bravery in other men, but he liked to hide his own exploits by telling stories against himself, of ridiculous mistakes and ludicrous accidents. Oddly enough, both these men had joined the army for the same reason —or so they said: not through poverty, like Sergeant Lawrence, or from family habit, like Mercer, but in the hope of glory and for the glamour of uniform. Each revealed himself in his recollection of this youthful vanity. 'How delightful on our return home,' Morris wrote, 'to parade the streets in our splendid uniforms, exhibiting ourselves as the brave defenders of our country'—and he meant it seriously. But Kincaid remembered his first march, when he tried to impress the natives (they were the natives of Kent) with his own importance 'by carrying a donkey-load of pistols in my belt, and screwing my naturally placid countenance up to a pitch of ferocity beyond what it was calculated to bear'.

At dawn, both these men were in characteristic form. Both were within 200 yards of Mercer, on the ridge above the farm and its orchard. Morris walked down to the farm and got some water, and while lesser men around him were complaining of cramps and agues, he shaved himself, with self-satisfaction, and put on a clean shirt. Kincaid, however, woke up to find that his horse had run away, and he had to spend most of the morning ignominiously asking, among about 10,000 other horses, if anyone had seen it.

*   *   *

One other man among those thousands must be introduced in that rainy summer dawn: an aide-de-camp of Sir Thomas Picton, fresh

Lieutenant Gronow

from the playing fields on which, the Duke said, the battle of Waterloo was won. This was Rees Howell Gronow. At the time when Mercer was digging for potatoes, he was on top of the ridge, in a tent made of muskets and blankets, eating cold ham and pie and drinking champagne for his breakfast—a feat which nobody, perhaps, except an old Etonian and officer of the Guards would have thought of achieving that morning.

Gronow ought not to have been there at all. Two battalions of his regiment were in the field, while his own was mounting guard at St. James's Palace. But scenting battle, he had persuaded Sir Thomas to take him to Belgium as an extra aide, had borrowed £200 and used it to win £600 at a gambling house in St. James's Square, and with that had bought an outfit he thought was suitable for an aide, including two first-rate horses from Tattersall's which he dispatched to Ostend with his groom. He arrived on the field much better turned out than his general with the rusty civilian hat. But Sir Thomas did not really need him, and the regiment had suffered badly at Quatre Bras, so he was sent to rejoin it. His friends in their bivouac greeted him with loud cries of 'How are you, old fellow? What the deuce brought you here? Take a glass of wine and a bit of ham. It will perhaps be your last breakfast.'

Gronow was not a man who looked like a fire-eating officer: small, dapper, fastidious and mannered, he wore—at least in later life—a tiny carefully barbered moustache and wavy luxuriant hair. Yet he became a celebrated duellist and was said to be the best pistol shot in the army: 'He committed the greatest follies,' it was said of him, 'without in the slightest disturbing the points of his shirt collar.' For the affectations of Regency beaux and dandies did not prevent them dashing to arms whenever a chance arose.

Gronow's family was among the landed gentry—their estates were in Glamorganshire—and any young man of his class with normal ambitions thought of the army: trade was unthinkable, the learned professions were a bore, but a short spell in the officers' mess of a crack regiment was a part of a gentleman's education and a passport to society. When Gronow was older he looked back with mild surprise at the total lack of training of Wellington's younger officers: he himself had been sent off to Spain in charge of a large detachment of troops when he was seventeen and only a few months out of school, and only the excellence of the non-commissioned officers, he said, had prevented fatal disasters in the face of the enemy. He never rose beyond the rank of captain, but that was simply because he did not care to buy any further promotion. For military rank was bought and sold, and any man of suitable birth could buy it, if he could afford it. Wellington himself had bought his way up to the rank of major before he had seen any active service at all, and at one time when he was broke he had seriously thought of selling his majority for the cash he needed. It was only in the higher ranks that experience and skill began to count.

People ever since those carefree days have wondered that this iniquitous system worked. For it did work: British officers were admired by foreign armies. The reason, in Wellington's opinion, was that officers were gentlemen: this was the main cause, he said, of the excellence of the British army at its best. Perhaps nobody ever defined the word gentleman, as it was used in the time of the Regency, but everybody, whether he was one or not, knew what it meant. It was not exclusively British—there were such things, in British eyes, as foreign gentlemen: but Wellington conspicuously was one, and Napoleon was definitely not. You could become an Emperor, but you could not possibly become a gentleman. You could buy the rank of major, but the quality of a gentleman was one thing you could not buy. Indeed, to aspire to being a gentleman if you were not was ungentlemanly in itself. 'A French officer,' Wellington once remarked, 'will cut your throat if you tell him he is not a gentleman, but that does not make him one.'

Thus Gronow, Leeke, Kincaid and Mercer were gentlemen, each in his own degree; Sergeants Wheeler, Lawrence and Morris were not, and even Morris, for all his self-esteem, would never have dreamed he could become one. Morris was a Londoner, but most Englishmen were still countrymen, and the gentry were still arbiters of country life. Labourers, tenants, farmers, shop-keepers, all treated their local gentry with unquestioning deference: in return, they expected, and usually received, advice, protection and help in adversity. Officers and men in Wellington's army were simply squire and tenant translated to a slightly different sphere. There were good squires and bad, of course, and there were good officers and bad: but an officer or a squire had to be very bad indeed to destroy the deeply traditional respect which lesser people gave to his position.

It worked because the peculiar qualities of a gentleman, being founded on an earlier code of chivalry, included all the qualities expected of an officer. He had an inborn habit of authority, and a very strict sense of what was fair. He had ridden a horse and handled a gun since he could walk. He had a sporting disregard for danger, which he cultivated on the hunting field. He was used to comfort at home, and so he could treat the passing discomfort of active service as a picnic. He could be rude, eccentric, occasionally angry, but he always treated his subordinates as men. And that was all a young officer needed. Mercer, in the artillery, had to have technical knowledge, but the technicalities of the cavalry and infantry were so simple that a bright young man could pick them up as he went along. And if he was not very bright, his colonel and probably even his major would know what to do, and his sergeant would know how to do it: and having been told, the young gentleman would do it, with an inimitable air.

* * *

Just before his champagne breakfast, Gronow had met the ultimate flower of this concept of the military gentleman. His own splendour was diminished. When his momentary career as an aide-de-camp came to an end, he had had to become a foot soldier again, and his first and only question was 'What the deuce shall I do with my horse?' Luckily, an officer bought the Tattersall's beauty there and then (the other had been left in Brussels): and as Gronow was delicately picking his way on foot up the road from Waterloo to the

The Duke and his staff emerging from the forest of Soignes

ridge, which was ankle deep in mud, he was overtaken by forty or fifty glittering horsemen: the Duke and his staff. They all seemed to him as gay and unconcerned as if they were riding to meet the hounds in some quiet English county.

The Duke led the cavalcade on his chestnut Copenhagen. He was wearing a dark blue coat and a cloak, a white cravat, white leather breeches and Hessian boots, and a cocked hat with four cockades—a mode of dress conspicuous by its plainness. As he passed he was chatting with the Duke of Richmond, who was an old friend of his but was not in the army and had only come to see the fun: and the Duke of Richmond was followed by his son Lord William Lennox, a boy of fifteen. There were Lord Fitzroy Somerset, his military secretary, and his eight aides-de-camp, the men who carried his orders on horseback through the army. There were General Müffling, the liaison officer of the Prussian commander Marshal Blücher, and the foreign attachés, princes, barons, counts and generals, men with resounding names and exotic uniforms. There were Lord Uxbridge, Lord Edward Somerset and Sir William Ponsonby of the cavalry, each with his aides; of the infantry commanders, Sir Thomas Picton, who had found his uniform, and Sir James Kempt, who was the man who had given Ensign Leeke his ginger biscuit. There were the twenty-two-year-old general, the Prince of Orange; Sir Edward Barnes, the Adjutant-General; and, at the end of the procession, the Quartermaster-General, Sir William De Lancey. The sun had risen, the rain had stopped, the army's sodden uniforms were steaming, and the Duke was bringing the orders it awaited: to stand and give battle.

MORNING

The decision to fight—The battlefield
The Emperor—The weapons

MORNING

Of all the staff, it was probably Sir William De Lancey who knew most about the events that had led to the Duke's decision. As Quartermaster-General, it had been his responsibility, two days before, to set the army on the move, dispatching his orderlies to ride through the night from Brussels with written orders. And although the movement had seemed chaotic to the soldiers who marched through the lanes, it had been successful: the whole army was now assembled on the ground the Duke had chosen for it.

De Lancey was a remarkable man, even in that remarkable company: young, brilliant, handsome and likeable. He was not one of the aristocrats who filled so many of the senior posts in the army. He was American. He was born in New York, where his Huguenot forebears had been distinguished citizens for over a hundred years, and he had been knighted when he was just over thirty for his service under Wellington in Spain. The Duke had insisted, in the face of strong opposition, on having De Lancey with him in Belgium, and had put him in his position of awesome responsibility although he was still only thirty-four.

The Duke's insistence would have flattered any man, but it cannot have been entirely welcome, for De Lancey was happily in love. The order to come at once to Belgium had reached him early in April at Dunglass on the coast of Scotland east of Edinburgh, where less than a week before he had married a Scottish girl named Magdalene Hall. The order allowed him no delay: he had had to leave his bride and post to London. But with the resourcefulness of love, she had contrived to follow him, and she had reached Brussels on 8 June. So there, they had spent a second week of their interrupted marriage. Each of its days had seemed to her like a gay and perfect dream, tinged by enough anxiety for the future to make the present intensely

Lady De Lancey

Sir William De Lancey

valuable. Entranced by each other's company, they had not attended any of the balls and dinner parties that Brussels offered every night: time had seemed too precious.

The idyll had ended on the evening of the 15th, when she fastened all his medals and crosses on his coat and helped him to put it on, because he had to call on the Spanish Ambassador. He did not want to go, and put it off as long as he could. When he had gone, she sat at the window, consciously grateful for her happiness, watching for his return. But at seven, she saw him gallop down the street to the Duke's house and run into it, leaving his horse in the middle of the road.

For two hours, she waited and worried. He had warned her already that when operations began he would be neglecting his duty if he thought for five minutes of anything else; so when at last he came back, she made him some strong green tea and did not ask any questions. But he told her briefly what had happened.

It was said afterwards that the Duke was already at the Duchess of Richmond's celebrated ball, which was held that evening, when he heard that Napoleon had advanced across the frontier. That was not so. He heard of it first by chance from the Prince of Orange, who had come to Brussels for the ball. The Duke was surprised to meet him, because he had posted him on the frontier with his troops to give early warning of any movement by the French. He asked him if there was any news. 'No,' the ingenuous Prince replied, 'nothing but that the French have crossed the Sambre and had a brush with the Prussians. Have you heard of it?' It was this information, so ludicrously given, that caused the sudden summons to De Lancey and set in train the movement of the army. A little later General Müffling, Marshal Blücher's representative, arrived with confirmation of the news, and De Lancey found him and the Duke conferring over a map, Müffling in full dress uniform and the Duke in his chemise and slippers, preparing to dress for the ball. 'I cannot tell the world,' the Duke said afterwards, 'that Blücher picked the fattest man in his army to ride with an express to me, and that he took thirty hours to go thirty miles.'

These were not the only sources of information that had failed. Of course, the British had spies in France who had been sending information of Napoleon's moves by the regular post-chaises from Paris to Brussels. But a few days before, the post-chaises had suddenly been stopped on the French side, and messages at the crucial moment had been delayed. Napoleon's spies in Belgium were impossible to detect. They could disguise themselves with ease among the multitude of foreign officers, many of whom wore uniforms of their own or their tailors' invention: one of Napoleon's generals attended the ball that night in a Belgian uniform and had the distinction of being greeted by the Duke, who shook his hand and said 'We shall have sharp work soon. I am glad to see you.' So, it was this multiple failure of his sources of information, rather than any trickery of Napoleon, which led to the Duke's more famous remark that night to the Duke of Richmond: 'Napoleon has humbugged me, by God.'

The Duke was criticized afterwards, by gossips who knew less than he did of the command of an army, for going to the ball. But this was nonsense. He finished dressing and went, after seeing General Müffling, because he thought that to stop the ball, or even to be absent himself, would alarm the aristocratic and somewhat feather-brained community of English who had followed the army to Brussels—it would have been bad if the army, starting to march to the south, had seen the civil gentry running away to the north.

Perhaps an added reason, and an equally good one, was that he wanted to go: he enjoyed that kind of glittering occasion, and most of his friends were going, including Lady Frances Webster, his love of the moment. Perhaps there was also something of a gesture in it, like Drake's game of bowls. But there was no need to look for reasons why he went: there was simply no reason why he should not go. He had told De Lancey, in whom he had complete faith, where and when he wanted his army assembled, and for the present that was all a commander-in-chief could do. It was De Lancey who had to work that festive evening.

While the cheerful music sounded down the street, and Scottish soldiers detailed for the job performed their Highland dances, and officers tried to bring their amorous adventures to a suitable conclusion, De Lancey sat writing the orders that sent the army out to meet Napoleon: and the only person with him was his wife, who had asked him to let her sit in the room and had promised not to speak. They were only interrupted by the aides and orderlies who came to take the movement orders as he completed them. Now and then, she gave him cups of tea, and felt herself rewarded by a grateful glance. By an effort of will, she hid her fear of the immediate future, and seemed to be calm. About two o'clock, he went to tell the Duke that the orders were finished and dispatched, but he found him in bed and asleep. At three, when the day was breaking, the troops who were assembled in the city began to march, and Sir William and Magdalene De Lancey leaned out of their window together and watched them pass, and listened to the bagpipes, fifes and bugles. Then he said she should go to Antwerp, and at six she endured the parting she had known must come.

*　　　*　　　*

On the information he possessed, the Duke could not do more than make an intelligent guess at Napoleon's point of attack: wherever the French first crossed the frontier, it might have been a feint. His first guess was too far to the west: he directed his army towards Enghien, twenty-five miles west of Quatre Bras. Some of his military critics in after years called this a blunder, arguing that Napoleon's obvious strategy was to separate the British and Prussian armies, and that an attack in the west would only have driven them

The troops began to march out of Brussels

together. But the Duke was not thinking of being driven anywhere. He thought Napoleon might try to draw him away to the west, and so to effect the separation. And in the event the guess was not too far wrong: he was able to bring enough of his forces back to Quatre Bras to hold Napoleon there for a day.

But in the forty-eight hours since the De Lanceys' parting, all the plans had been changed, because the Prussians' defeat at Ligny had obliged the Duke to retreat from Quatre Bras. During the miserable night that the troops spent out in the rain, it was not only they who were wondering whether they would stand and fight, or retreat again: he himself had not made up his mind. The evening before, Lord Uxbridge, as the next senior British officer (the Duke had no recognized second-in-command), had asked him what he meant to do. 'Buonaparte has not given me any idea of his projects,' the Duke replied irritably, 'and as my plans will depend on his, how can you expect me to tell you what mine are?' Five years before, Lord Uxbridge had fallen in love with the Duke's sister-in-law and involved both her and himself in scandalous divorces, so people expected a certain coolness between the two commanders; but the Duke made up for that particular snub by adding a little more kindly, 'There is one thing certain, Uxbridge; that is that whatever happens, you and I will do our duty.'

But it was not entirely on Napoleon's plans that the Duke's depended, it was also on Marshal Blücher's. The Duke did not feel strong enough to stop Napoleon on the road to Brussels unless he could count on Prussian help. The Prussian army at Ligny, in his own words, had been damnably mauled, and the intrepid old marshal himself, who was seventy-two, had been rolled on by his horse and only rescued, badly bruised and shaken, after two cavalry charges, one French and one his own, had passed over him where he lay. The Duke had sent him messages, saying he would fight at Waterloo if he could count on the help of one Prussian corps: if not, he expected to have to abandon Brussels and retreat beyond the Scheldt. At two o'clock in the morning, in the inn he had requisitioned in Waterloo, this drastic choice was still in front of him—and that was almost the hour when the retreat, if it was to be retreat, would have to be ordered. It was not until then that a Prussian aide came riding in with Blücher's answer. It was addressed to Müffling. 'Your Excellency will assure the Duke of Wellington from me that,

ill as I am, I shall place myself at the head of my troops, and attack
the right of the French, in case they undertake anything against his
Grace. If, on the other hand, the day should pass without their
making any attack, it is then my opinion that we should jointly
attack them tomorrow.'

It was a brave answer. Blücher's chief of staff, General Gneisenau,
rather spoilt it by adding a covering letter: he was known to dislike
and mistrust the Duke, and told Müffling to find out whether the
Duke really meant to fight, or only to make a demonstration. And
since the nearest surviving part of Blücher's army was at the village
of Wavre, ten miles away as the crow flies to the east, it was clear
they could not arrive until the day was well advanced.

But on that assurance, the Duke decided to fight. He wrote letters
to the French royalists, whose headquarters were in Ghent, to the

'*The perilous situation of Marshal Blücher at the Battle of Ligny*'

authorities in Brussels, and to Lady Frances Webster. He advised the
French and the British to make preparations for retreat, although he
hoped all would be well; but he suggested to Lady Frances that she
should leave Brussels at once and go to Antwerp. Then he lay down
and slept. 'I don't like lying awake, it does no good,' he said when
he was older. 'I make a point never to lie awake.'

*   *   *

Thus, when the Duke and his staff, so gay and unconcerned, rode
out from Waterloo in the morning, the decision to fight was only
four hours old. But he knew the ground he was to fight on. The
ridge where the army was waiting was two and a half miles south
of the village. He had seen it before, and decided already that it was
the best defensive position on the road to Brussels. On his orders, the
staff had prepared a sketch map of it and two copies had been made:
the Prince of Orange had one, and De Lancey, at the rear of the
cavalcade, was carrying the other in his pocket.

The road from Brussels and Waterloo, south towards Charleroi
and the border of France, climbed by a hardly perceptible gradient
through the forest of Soignes, past hamlets with the pleasant names
of Vieux-Amis and Joli-Bois. Where it emerged at last from the
outlying woods of the forest, there was a tiny cluster of cottages
called Mont St. Jean, and another main road forked off to the right,
towards Nivelles. On the left, beyond the fork, was a large farm,
also called Mont St. Jean, with massive buildings round a yard which
was reached through an archway from the road. Beyond the farm
the main road was crossed by a lane: and it was there, at the crossroads, that the road suddenly dipped a little ahead, and a traveller,
for the first time since he left Brussels, had an open view across a
shallow valley. The road ran perfectly straight across the valley and
rose on the other side, a little over half a mile away, to an inn on the
skyline which was called La Belle Alliance, to commemorate the
unromantic but profitable marriage of its owner.

On the left of the road, the valley grew deeper until it disappeared
behind a curve of the ridge. But on the right, it divided into a
confusing mass of small valleys, mere folds in the open fields, some
so shallow that a horseman in one would hardly be hidden from
a horseman in the next. Here and there in the valley were fields of

Where the road emerged from the forest, stood a cluster of cottages called Mont St. Jean

clover, but most of it, on that June morning, was covered by a crop of rye which had grown as high as a man, so that sometimes a column of soldiers marching through it in single file could only be seen by the muzzles of their muskets, and their bayonets glittering in the sun. After the pouring rain of the night, the whole valley was muddy, especially where the troops in their bivouacs had trampled down the crop: the sandy soil of that part of Belgium makes exceptionally slimy, slippery mud.

The lane which crossed the main road at the top of the hill followed exactly the crest of the ridge in both directions: and it was

From the crossroad, the road ran straight across the valley, past La Haye Sainte, to La Belle Alliance on the skyline

this lane that the Duke had chosen as his front line. For a hundred yards or so, the main road was sunk in a cutting where it crossed the ridge, and the lane also descended into it by cuttings on each side. Close to the crossroads, they were ten or fifteen feet deep, and the one on the right continued most of the way to the other main road, the road to Nivelles. But on the left, the lane soon levelled off. It had holly hedges on both sides. On its right, the ground fell away to the valley, and a man standing on the lane, or behind the hedges, could see most of the valley below him: not quite all of it, because there were undulations all over the valley bottom.

Three groups of buildings stood among the sodden ryefields in the valley, each of them to be garrisoned as an outpost. The first, on the far left, a mile from the main road, was a farm called Papelotte. The second was the farm of La Haye Sainte, in whose orchard Mercer had spent the night. That was on the right-hand side of the main road itself, 200 yards below the crossroads. The third and most isolated was a small château called Hougoumont, out of sight from the crossroads beyond the rolling country on the right. That morning, the inhabitants of all those places had fled, with two exceptions.

The valley from the ridge with La Haye Sainte on the left (just below the Duke's position)

The farmer's wife of Mont St. Jean, behind Wellington's ridge, stayed all day in an attic of the farm, through shot and shell, explaining that she could not leave her animals. And the gardener at Hougoumont stayed to look after his garden until it was filled and surrounded by battling troops and he could not escape.

When the Duke and his staff reached the crossroads, they turned a few yards down the lane to the right and climbed out of the cutting. As they put their horses one by one at the slippery bank, the popping of musketry could be heard from the fields all round them, sounding almost as if a battle had begun. But this was only the infantry, clearing the charges that had lain in their muskets all night —a tedious job if you did it as it had to be done in barracks, but easy if you fired your musket into the air. The Duke and the staff took up a position he had chosen in front of an elm tree in the angle of the main road and the lane. From there, on horseback, he could see down the valley to the left, across the road. To the right, his view was more restricted, and in front it was partly obscured by the roofs of the house and farm buildings of La Haye Sainte. It was not a perfect point of observation, but it was the best there was. From it, one by one, the generals rode away, and then the aides-de-camp, taking his orders to commanders who had not been in his company. All over the ridge and down the valley, the drums began to sound the call to arms, and the army began to move, to take up its battle line.[1]

*   *   *

The movements the Duke had ordered answered one of the questions the army had been asking: if the French came on, they were to fight them. But that was all that the orders implied. It was not his way to tell his men any more than they had to know, or to try to inspire them with flamboyant Orders of the Day. Most men saw him as he rode here and there along the ridge, observing and sometimes directing the movements. But few of them cheered. Men did not cheer the Duke: they respected, trusted and admired him, but they did not particularly like him, and if they tried to demonstrate any emotional feeling for him, he ignored it or put a stop to it. ('I hate to hear that cheering,' he said at a review a few weeks later. 'If once you allow soldiers to express an opinion, they may on some other occasion hiss instead of cheer.') To most soldiers, the orders seemed merely a matter of trudging from one patch of mud to another. There was no excitement about it, and not much noise when the drums had died away. Even the hum of conversation had stopped: men were hiding their feelings, whatever they were. Sergeant Wheeler and his regiment marched from their field at

[1] The first thing a modern visitor sees on the ridge is a huge pyramid with a lion on top, between the two main roads. This immense folly was built by the Belgians in the 1820s. To build it, they dug away all the soil on the south side of the lane, as far as the crossroads itself, to a depth of about six feet, and so destroyed the most interesting part of the battlefield they meant to commemorate. But just south of the crossroads there is a more modest memorial which was erected earlier. It stands now on a mound of earth, and the top of that mound is the original ground level. Near the pyramid there are car parks, restaurants, snack bars and souvenir shops, but the rest of the battlefield is very little changed. La Haye Sainte and part of Hougoumont were repaired after the battle, and among their buildings one can still follow the furious fighting which reduced them both to ruins that afternoon. The tree by the crossroads survived the battle and was known afterwards as the Wellington Tree, but it was mutilated by sightseers who cut off small pieces as souvenirs. In 1818 the remains of the tree were bought by an Englishman and carved into a chair, now in the possession of H.M. the Queen.

Waterloo to another field far on the right of the army, near the road to Nivelles. They piled their arms, but were told not to move away. Ensign Leeke and the 52nd Foot, who had woken up in the head of the valley at dawn, not far from the hedge of the orchard of Hougoumont, marched a couple of hundred yards up the ridge and over it, and stood to their arms on the other side. Captain Kincaid of the Rifles did not move at all—he was already on the lane immediately to the left of the crossroads—but he watched other units, which had camped on the slope of the valley in front of him, moving away until the valley was empty and there was nobody between him and the enemy. He found his horse, and in their central position, he and his men made a huge camp kettle of tea: all the big-wigs in the army from the Duke downwards, it seemed to him, came past in the early part of the morning and asked for a cup. Nor did Mercer move—but that was only because his senior officers had forgotten him, hidden with his troop in the orchard down the road. Gronow and his regiment of the Guards marched up from the edge of the forest to the lane on the right of the crossroads, and he was one of the few who happened to halt in a place where he could see along the ridge. To him, it looked like a continuous wall of human beings.

It was a good enough description. Troops in those days stood literally shoulder to shoulder in their battle lines; 21 inches was the standard interval for infantry, and 36 inches for cavalry. The army was not yet in line, but the infantry was disposed behind the ridge so that when it did extend into line it would form two continuous ranks all the way from the Nivelles road to a point above the farm of Papelotte, a distance of roughly two miles. Artillery was placed between the regiments of infantry, and the reserves, with the whole of the cavalry, were farther back between the ridge and the edge of the forest.

This was the conventional disposition for defence. But most of the British infantry noticed with misgiving that they had a foreign regiment on each side of them. If they had put two and two together, they might have deduced that the Duke was making the most of his mixed collection of men by putting British and foreigners alternately along the line. And if they had had a map, or any clear idea of the lie of the land, they might have noticed another innovation. Since time immemorial, army commanders had drawn up their troops in view of the enemy, to display their strength. But in Spain the Duke had learned from his own experience that this was foolishly dangerous in the face of modern artillery, and he had made a practice of keeping his troops out of sight. He was doing it again at Waterloo. The mass of the infantry was over the top of the ridge, on the gentle northern slope, where they would not offer a visible target to Napoleon's gunners.

Consequently, only a few of them could see what was happening on the far side of the valley. Those who could—Gronow and Kincaid were among them—relieved the boredom of waiting by watching with mild interest a display of military pomp which was clearly visible through the rain-washed air. 'There he is on his white horse!' said one of Gronow's companions who happened to have a spy-glass: and everyone knew whom he meant.

*　　　*　　　*

The Emperor had slept at a farmhouse called Le Caillou, on the main road, two miles south of Wellington's army, and at about eight o'clock breakfast was served to him there on the imperial silver plate. He intended to sleep the following night at the Palace of Laeken in Brussels, but before he left Le Caillou he ordered a leg of mutton for his dinner, and men of his staff, on the lookout for auguries, concluded that the entry into Brussels would be late. About nine, he called for his horses and rode up to La Belle Alliance to observe the British position. Two Belgian peasants had been persuaded to help him with their local knowledge. One of them stayed with his staff all day, but the other shook so much in the Emperor's presence that he could not speak a word, so he was allowed to go home; and when he was asked afterwards what the Emperor was like, he made the charmingly zany answer: 'If his face was the face of a clock, nobody would dare to look at it to tell the time.'

The Emperor's columns were marching up the road and beginning to take their places for the battle, and as they approached, deployed and halted, he passed them in review. In the memory of those who played their part, this was a scene of military splendour never surpassed and never to be repeated, a totally different thing from the bored assembly preoccupied with its own discomfort which faced it across the valley.

The Duke of Wellington

Here, marching with the rest, one man among 70,000, came Pierre Robinaux, a captain of infantry, a man who was humble by nature and yet was intensely proud to share in this moment of exaltation.

In Wellington's army there was no such thing as a typical soldier, but in Napoleon's there was: one could truthfully say that Captain Robinaux was typical, and so his feelings have a special significance. Robinaux, multiplied by 70,000, was the strength of Napoleon's army. He was thirty-one, and had served in the army since he was twenty, an amiable man, fond of a glass of wine, a good companion; perhaps a little too precise in his thoughts and not very imaginative —but long service in any army might make a man like that. He had had a reward for his service that would have been rare among the British: he was only a peasant by birth, unpretentious and not highly educated, and he had started as an ordinary conscript, but he had been promoted from the ranks simply because he was an excellent

soldier. At first he had been miserable and homesick for his father's farm, but after a while the army had become his home, and army life the only life he wanted. In his eleven years, he had only once been back to the farm on leave, and had never had time for romance. He had fought in twenty major battles and more skirmishes than he had bothered to count, and he had marched, continuously, month after month, summer and winter, thousands and thousands of miles all over Europe, making a home in bivouacs in the rain of north Germany, the snow of Austria, or the summer sun of Italy. He had never grumbled and never complained, and since his early days he had never even felt sorry for himself, because he had always felt honoured to serve the Emperor, and privileged to take a share, however small, in the glory of his victories.

Robinaux might have hesitated to say that he worshipped the Emperor: he was a Christian, like any French peasant. But there was really no other word for his feeling. The Emperor was his God on earth, more present than the God in heaven. In his eyes, the Emperor was wiser, more powerful, more distant, more stern and more just than any mere human could be. The Emperor did no wrong: disasters like Moscow, in Robinaux's mind, had other explanations. Robinaux thought himself blessed to live not only in the time but in the country of the Emperor, and he had sincerely devoted his life to him with the passion of a saint or a lover. He had welcomed privation and suffering for his sake, and had proved already, hundreds of times, that he was willing to die for him. He looked for nothing in life, or in death, except the reflection of the Emperor's glory.

When the Emperor fell and was exiled to Elba, the mainspring of Robinaux's life was abruptly broken: he did not know of anything else to live for. But those ten months of aimless misery had only added to the ecstasy of the return, and of marching out again on a new campaign. Already, at Ligny, the Emperor had proved that glory was not a thing of the past, but a thing of the present and future. So now, as Robinaux marched with his 70,000 companions in all the panoply of the imperial might, his heart swelled in an access of pride and adoration. He put his shako on the point of his sword and waved it, and shouted again and again '*Vive l'Empereur!*' So did they all.

'It was a kaleidoscope of vivid hues and metallic flashes,' the French historian Henry Houssaye wrote of that parade. 'After the chasseurs, wearing bright green jackets, with facings of purple, yellow or scarlet, came the hussars, with dolmans, pelisses, breeches à la hongroise, plumes upon their shakos, all varying in colour with each regiment. . . . Then passed the dragoons with brass casques over turban-helmets of tiger skin, white shoulder belts crossed over a green coat with facings of red or yellow, long guns at their saddle bows and bumping against their stiff boots; the cuirassiers wearing short coats with Imperial blue collars, white breeches, top boots, steel cuirasses and helmets, with crests of copper and floating horse-hair manes; the carabiniers, giants of six feet and clad in white, with breastplates of gold and tall helmets 'with red cords—like those worn by the heroes of antiquity. And now the entire body of the horse guards deployed on the third line; the dragoons in green coats faced with white and with scarlet plumes on their helmets; the grenadiers in blue coats faced with scarlet, leather breeches and high caps of

Officer of the Chasseurs à cheval

bearskin, with a plume and hanging cords; the lancers with red kurkas and blue plastrons, with light yellow aiguillettes and epaulettes, red trousers with a blue stripe, and the red shapka cap bearing a brass plate inscribed with an N and a crown, and surmounted with a white plume half a yard long; and last the chasseurs, with green dolmans embroidered with orange braid, red pelisses edged with fur and kilbachs [or caps] of brilliant scarlet, with great plumes of green and red upon their heads. The epaulettes, the braids, the stripes, the gimps of the officers glittered with a profuse display of gold and silver.'

'The earth seemed proud to bear so many brave men,' Napoleon wrote in one of his flights of fancy at St. Helena. 'The whole formed a magnificent spectacle, and must have struck the enemy with awe.' On and on they came, men, horses and cannon as far as the eye could reach—the foot artillery men in their bearskin helmets marching beside the twelve-pounder guns which the Emperor called his most beautiful daughters—each regiment seeming to outdo the last in the gaudy fantasy of its plumage, with the single exception of the Emperor's Old Guard, the élite of them all, who came far in the rear in their plain campaigning dress, blue trousers and greatcoats and plain bearskins without either plumes or braid—for they were carrying their parade uniforms in their knapsacks ready for the triumphal entry into Brussels.

Drums beat, the trumpets sounded, the bands of every regiment shook the air—'*Veillons au salut de l'Empire!*': and passing before Napoleon, the eagle-bearers inclined the new standards he had presented, standards 'baptized by fire and blood' at Ligny, the cavalry brandished their sabres, the infantry waved their caps on the points of their bayonets, and the cheers drowned the officers' words of command and were carried on the breeze across the valley to the sceptical spectators on the other side, who were far less impressed than Napoleon believed: Kincaid, for example, who dourly said, 'It looked as if they had some hopes of scaring us off the ground.'

This was the scene in memory, and possibly nobody in Napoleon's host escaped its intoxication or observed it with detachment. Men were hypnotized by the martial music and their own accoutrements. Uniforms in every army, beyond their mundane use of distinguishing friend from foe, were designed to make a man feel stronger, bigger and braver than he was, and to make his friends and enemies feel it too.[1] The helmets, bearskins and plumes made him taller—all military hats were high—epaulettes made narrow shoulders broader, padded tunics swelled a narrow chest; and the garish colours and glittering decorations enhanced his virile pride, and helped him to forget the vulnerable human body inside its pathetic disguise.

In their exalted state of mind, none of them noticed, or all of them forgot, that most of the splendid uniforms were smeared from plumes to boots in mud. But in sober fact, these men, so elegant in retrospect, had not taken off their clothes for nearly a week and, excepting the staff, were all bedraggled by spending the night like the British, lying in muddy fields under the teeming rain. One of them, remembering that night, said the mud was as soft as a feather bed to lie on; and it was a satisfaction, he added, to know that whenever you turned over, the side that had lain in the mud would be washed by the rain.

This man was a young officer of infantry named Martin. Although he was a graduate of the military College of Saint-Cyr, he did retain —perhaps because he was Swiss—some independence in his judgement. Even he was deeply impressed by the scene. It seemed to him even more imposing and solemn because he could see, a thousand yards away, the long line of red on the top of the British ridge. His regiment took its place just on the right of the main road in front of La Belle Alliance. It was a position exactly opposite Kincaid's; and Kincaid was a man he might have understood, because both of them had a sense of humour which made them laugh in the most unlikely circumstances. While they formed up, he was wondering why they had started so late in the morning. In his regiment, every man had been awake and out of his muddy bed by daylight. They had made fires and hastily grilled some pieces of beef for breakfast—it seemed delicious—and then they had expected to move at once, to continue their advance and force the British to continue their retreat. But four or five hours had passed, and they had been left without orders, doing nothing.

The same kind of delay had surprised him the day before. The regiment then had been ready to move at dawn, facing the battlefield of Quatre Bras. But all that morning too—the morning when Mercer, equally surprised, had waited for the attack—they had stood without orders. And when at last the orders came, in the afternoon,

[1] On parade, they still are.

the British had gone and the battlefield was deserted, except for its corpses. Among those, to his astonishment, he saw some dead soldiers wearing skirts: he had never heard before of Scottish customs.

*   *   *

The delays on those two mornings, which were strange enough to puzzle such junior officers as Martin and Mercer, have been argued about ever since. What had happened to Napoleon? The veterans of the Grand Army who led the ecstatic cheers, the men like Captain Robinaux, had faith that was unshakeable. But his marshals and senior generals saw a change. One of them said 'The Napoleon we knew does not exist any more', and the suspicion that something was seriously wrong with him confused them and undermined their confidence, not only in him but in themselves and in each other.

Diagnoses of his state of mind and body have been an entertainment for doctors ever since. He was only forty-five, three months younger than Wellington; but during the past three years he had suddenly grown fat, and that has been read as a symptom of a pituitary disorder which might also have blurred the sharpness of his brain. This might have caused the lack of decision and clarity which can certainly be seen in his written orders during his last campaign, and the fits of drowsiness and lethargy which are said to have overcome him.

But discussion of his health has always been obscured by partisan emotion. Some people delight in finding mundane ills in men of high repute. On the other hand, some Bonapartists exaggerated his illnesses to explain or excuse his mistakes; some hated to admit that his actions could ever have been influenced by illness; others, including himself, always denied that he made mistakes at all. From all the discussion, one reasonably certain fact remains: that in the night after Ligny, the Emperor had an acute attack of piles.

He had been on horseback most of the day. In the evening he left the battlefield and went back to his headquarters without giving any orders for pursuing the beaten Prussians. Marshal Grouchy, who had led his forces, followed him to ask for orders, but was told Napoleon was indisposed. He went again at dawn, but Napoleon would not see him. At nine in the morning, Napoleon sent an inconclusive dispatch to Marshal Ney, who was facing Wellington at Quatre

Napoleon: from a portrait painted shortly before the battle

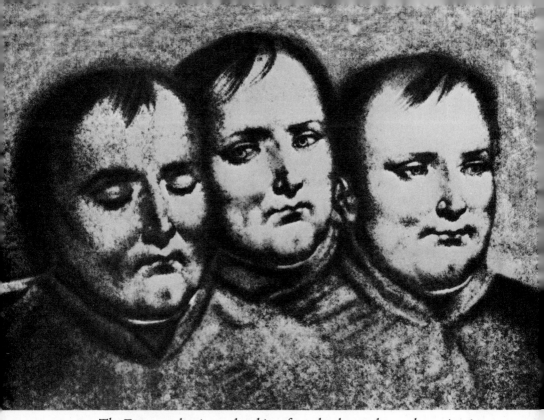

The Emperor, sleeping and waking, from sketches made at a theatre in 1812

Bras, and then he went back to Ligny, where he inspected the battle-field of the day before, talked to the wounded and chatted to his entourage—not about the urgent military action that was needed, but about the political situation in Paris. When Grouchy ventured to ask again for orders he answered curtly 'I will give them to you when I think fit.' At about half past eleven, he suddenly seemed to recover himself, but by then both Wellington and Blücher had with-drawn their forces out of his reach. That afternoon, he rode to Quatre Bras—where Mercer saw him—and he was well up with the van of his army all through the pursuit to the position at Waterloo.

Only three other people are thought to have known what had happened in the night: Napoleon always took care to hide his own ailments from his troops, and even though people were perhaps less prudish then, to suffer from piles was not a dignified mishap. The three were his brother Prince Jerome, his doctor Baron Larrey, who had served him for twenty years, and his valet Marchand, who had shared the exile in Elba; and it was only Jerome who revealed the secret, years after the Emperor's death. He had had piles for the past two years, and was often constipated too. His own remedy was to apply leeches to the affected part, but Larrey had a lotion that he recommended. In an acute attack, the piles would no doubt have prolapsed and become extremely painful. Yet he was in the saddle again for most of another day.

That may not have been his only suffering. Jerome's revelation was not made public until 1900, and French historians of the 19th century could only offer the hints or guesses of people who observed the Emperor that day. One of them said he had an inflammation which made the saddle painful: another mentioned two separate ailments, without saying what they were. And Houssaye, at the end of the century, pointed out that the Emperor must have been very tired, and then admitted an added possibility: that he had

Prince Jerome

an attack of cystitis. It was that inflammation of the bladder and urinary tract that had put him out of action at the battle of Borodino; he suffered from it many times before and afterwards, and it was found as a chronic condition in the post-mortem dissection at St. Helena. It seemed to be brought on in acute attacks by cold and wet—and during the pursuit to Waterloo, the Emperor was soaked to the skin like everybody else. Cystitis can cause a high fever, and can also be very painful, with a constant need to pass water and acute pain when one does so—a pain which can absorb an ordinary patient's attention and make him unable to concentrate his mind on anything else. If Houssaye's supposition was true, the piles had started on the night after Ligny, and the cystitis on the day after Quatre Bras, and the Emperor, on the day of Waterloo, was suffering both these crippling kinds of pain and possibly had a fever—yet still had to try to direct his army, to force himself to think and be active, and to hide the pain and indignity from the thousands of men who were watching him. Perhaps his brain was chronically less sharp than it had been: that must always remain a mere hypothesis. But whether it was or not, the passing effects of piles, cystitis and weariness are enough to account for everything he did or failed to do. He behaved that day like a sick man preoccupied with pain.

In St. Helena, when he had nothing else to do, Napoleon took a great interest in his own ailments, but he never confessed to anyone that he felt ill at Waterloo: that might have seemed an admission that he was to blame, a thing he never admitted. He did say that in his last campaign his old confidence had deserted him. That morning, while the armies waited and he seemed to struggle with his physical distress, his words and actions suggested the opposite: that he was illogically over-confident. But perhaps he was making a display of confidence, to hide his own doubts from his generals, or even from himself.

He is said to have risen at dawn, but he did not confer with his generals or leave the farmhouse of Le Caillou until he had had his breakfast four hours later. When he had eaten, the table was cleared and maps were spread on it, and in the next hour all the highest commanders of the army came and went. 'We have ninety chances in our favour,' the Emperor said, 'and not ten against us.' And to Marshal Ney, who came in from the outposts and said he thought

Wellington was preparing to retreat, he insisted: 'You have seen wrong. Wellington has thrown the dice and they are in our favour.'

Napoleon himself had never fought Wellington, but some of his generals had. Marshal Soult, his Chief of Staff, urged him to bring back the 33,000 men under Marshal Grouchy who were still on the Prussians' line of retreat from Ligny, fifteen miles away to the east. 'Because you have been beaten by Wellington, you think him a great general,' Napoleon said with more than his usual brusqueness. 'I tell you Wellington is a bad general, the English are bad troops, and this affair is nothing more than a picnic.' Another officer with experience of the British in Spain said he believed the British infantry was impregnable in a frontal attack and could only be defeated by manœuvre, because of its calm tenacity and superior aim in firing. But Napoleon dismissed that opinion with a mere exclamation of disbelief.

Prince Jerome also came into Le Caillou with a piece of gossip that he thought deserved a hearing. The evening before, he had had his supper at an inn down the road where Wellington had had his breakfast. The waiter who served them both told Jerome he had listened to the breakfast conversation, and had heard an aide-de-camp say that the British and Prussians had agreed to meet at the edge of the forest of Soignes. If the story was accurate, the aide-de-camp had been talking prematurely, as well as carelessly: at that time, the Duke had asked Blücher to send a Prussian corps, but had not yet received an answer. The story might have opened Napoleon's eyes to the possibility, but all he said when Jerome told him was: 'That is nonsense. A junction between them is impossible for at least two days.' And in spite of the doubt and hesitation of everyone around him, he refused to consider anything but a frontal attack, and did nothing to recall Marshal Grouchy and his forces. Outside Le Caillou, two generals spoke of pressing their advice. 'What is the use?' one of them said. 'He would not listen.'

By the time Napoleon had left Le Caillou and reviewed his troops nearly half the summer day had passed. Yet still, he seemed unable to force his mind to any fresh decision, either to order the battle to begin, or to move his army to out-manœuvre Wellington, or to order Grouchy to return. But what was he to do? It seems likely he knew, in the back of his mind, that he was too ill to direct a major battle efficiently that day. But the battle could not be avoided or postponed, and it was unthinkable that he should say he was ill and delegate the command to anybody else. Even if his own pride had allowed it, the effect on his army's morale would have been disastrous. So, subconsciously perhaps, he rejected every reason for haste or for positive action, and grasped the only reason for delay: the only advice he accepted that morning was from his artillery commanders, who said the ground was so wet it would be difficult to move the guns immediately, but that it was drying every hour. Such an excuse would have had short shrift from the old Napoleon. But it gave him a chance to rest. He rode back to another small inn, called Rossomme, three-quarters of a mile down the road between La Belle Alliance and Le Caillou. His servants brought an armchair and a table out of the building and put them on a little knoll beside the road, and spread some dry straw on the ground around them. The Emperor dismounted and sat for a long time with his elbows on his knees and his head in his hands. At a respectful distance, his staff awaited his commands. One of them, watching him, thought he was in a stupor.

*   *   *

By that time, eleven o'clock in the morning, 140,000 men—73,000 of his own and 67,000 of Wellington's—were waiting for his decision on the opposite sides of the valley. Among his own men, the ecstasy of the review was fading and the cheering had died away: among the British and their allies, or at least among those who had heard that the Prussians were coming, surprise at his inactivity was growing: for them, the longer he put it off the better. All over the field, men stood silent in their ranks, or sat on the ground in desultory conversation, or lay dozing with their heads on their knapsacks. After the cold, wet night, everyone was grateful for the sun. A kind of peace, a sense of lethargy descended, and men's thoughts strayed away to happier scenes and people far away, mothers, lovers and homes. Old soldiers told boastful stories to new recruits, who did not want to listen. It began to be hard to believe that the calm of the summer's day would be broken: yet everyone knew there was no retreat, that before the sun went down there must be slaughter and chaos in the quiet fields. Men's spirits sank with the waiting, and they secretly

The Infantry

looked at each other and wondered which would die. But whatever his private feelings nobody could admit he was afraid.

All of those thousands of patient men had one thing in common: each of them understood his own weapon, and more or less understood the battle drill and tactics of using it. And one cannot understand the men without knowing a little of that important part of what they knew.

Of the three arms, cavalry, artillery and infantry, the infantry were much the most numerous. The men of Ensign Leeke, and Sergeants Wheeler and Lawrence, carried the celebrated British musket called Brown Bess. It was already something of an antique: it had changed very little in the past 150 years. It fired an iron ball three-quarters of an inch in diameter. Its powder was carried in paper cartridges. To load it, you bit off the end of the cartridge and poured a little of the powder in the firing pan, and the rest down the barrel. Then you put the ball and wadding down the muzzle and rammed it all tight with the ramrod. In an emergency, it could be rammed by banging the butt on the ground, but that only worked if the ground was hard. A well-trained man could load and fire two shots a minute, but after about fifty shots the flint which ignited the powder wore out. As powder clogged the barrel, ramming became progressively more difficult, until you were forced to stop to clean the barrel out. You had to stand up to load the musket, and therefore you usually fired it standing. A musket-ball could be lethal at several hundred yards, but it needed more luck than skill to hit a man, or even a whole rank of men, much over seventy or eighty yards away. For closer, quicker work, you used the bayonet.

The rifles of Kincaid's men were a comparatively new and rare invention: they were called Baker's Rifle, and had only been used in the army since 1800. Their loading was slower, because it was harder to drive the ball and the ramrod down the barrel. But the rifling made them more accurate, and the men of the Rifle Brigade were regarded as the sharpshooters of the army.

Lord Uxbridge's cavalry were armed with sabres, and with carbines and pistols. Each cut and thrust of the sabre was numbered and listed in gruesome detail in the drill books. Among the Belgian cavalry, and among the French, there were also lancers, with weapons that had not changed since medieval times: some cavalrymen admitted that the lance, though less artistic than the sabre, was often more efficient, because it had a longer reach. The only armour, apart from helmets, was worn by the French cuirassiers: their

The Cavalry

pigeon-breasted steel cuirasses were proof against any but the subtlest sabre work, and sometimes they turned musket-balls aside. But, like all armour, they had the disadvantage of being cumbersome and heavy, especially when their wearers were unhorsed.

Last, there was the artillery: horse artillery, which was mobile, and something of a British speciality, and foot artillery, which took up a commanding position before a battle and seldom moved from it. Mercer's battery was of nine-pounders. Other cannon ranged from four- to twelve-pounders, and they fired three kinds of missile. Round-shot, a solid iron ball, was destructive through its momentum. One shot that afternoon was seen to knock over twenty-five men, one after another, and kill or wound them all: and even when a ball was rolling along the ground at the end of its range, it could take off a foot as it went. You could see a round-shot in flight if it was coming straight at you, but it was considered cowardly to duck; and you could see it easily when it began to bounce, ploughing up the earth each time it fell.

The shells of the artillery were also round. Being hollow and lighter, they did not bounce so much. If they had not exploded before they fell, they lay on the ground with their fuses fizzing and spluttering until the explosion came. Sportsmen sometimes picked them up and threw them away like cricket balls.

The third kind of shot was grape, canister or case. These were slight variations on the same principle: large numbers of musket-balls or scraps of iron, clamped together or packed in canvas bags which burst open when they were fired. The French at Waterloo were said to be using canister filled with horse-shoe nails. This was the artillery's short-range weapon, and a well-timed shot could mow down a whole rank of men or horses.

All the guns were aimed by turning the whole gun on its wheels until it pointed in the right direction, and estimating the range and elevation with a practised eye. None of them had any mechanism for absorbing recoil, and so they moved at every shot and had to be aimed again. The principles of loading and firing were much the same as the musket's, except that the powder was fired by a slow match instead of a flint, which the gunners kept burning all through a battle. The barrels had to be kept clean with wet sponges fixed on wooden staves. But with skill and energy, the rate of fire of artillery guns was about the same as the musket's, two shots a minute.

Neither cavalry, artillery nor infantry was invincible, and their interaction made a battle like a game of chess played by the rival commanders. Nowadays, to see the sense in the curiously formal moves, one constantly has to remind oneself that no weapon in those days could be accurately aimed. Musketry and artillery were only useful in the mass: if you fired a big enough volley, some of the shots would probably hit the target. If you yourself were shot on the battlefield, it was highly unlikely that the shot had been aimed at you as an individual: the risk was mainly from the quantity of shot which aimlessly flew around from the tens of thousands of weapons. So the Duke could ride up and down observing the enemy, and in full view of them: he ran a great risk of being shot, but very little risk from being deliberately shot at. So also officers, mounted and conspicuously dressed, could lead the infantry right up to the enemy bayonets. In the height of the battle, Mercer sat on his horse in front of his battery to encourage his men, and exchanged spoken insults with a French musketeer who was carefully taking aim at him: the man took his time, and Mercer wished he had never begun such a

Mercer's troop

show of bravery, but when the shot came it missed him. And as a battle progressed, any kind of aim became more difficult because the gunpowder made a thick blue-grey smoke, and your glimpses of the enemy depended on the eddies of the wind.

With this in mind, one can understand the tactics of the day. The only men who fought as individuals were the skirmishers, who were sent out in front of the army with muskets: they made use of whatever natural cover they could find, and kept up a fire which was meant to distract and annoy the enemy: 'those impudent popping fellows', somebody called them. The main body of the infantry fought in ranks. The drill which is still used on parade grounds as a ceremony and a kind of discipline was the basis then of battlefield manœuvres: units advanced and retreated over the open fields in ranks and columns, turned, wheeled and formed fours on their officers' words of command. As units, they could fire a volley which did some damage, and could defend themselves where a single man could not. They only broke their formations in bayonet charges, and after those they formed again as soon as they could for self-protection.

Against advancing infantry, they formed in line, because in that formation they could discharge the biggest simultaneous volleys. Traditionally, the lines were three deep, on the theory that the front rank would have re-loaded by the time the second and third had fired their volleys. That was still the practice in the French army, but in Spain the British had reduced the ranks to two, because the fire of the third rank was always more or less impeded by the two in front.

These extended lines were also the best defence against long-range artillery, in so far as a cannon shot passing through them was unlikely to kill more than two men. But they were powerless to stop a cavalry charge, and on the word 'Prepare to receive cavalry', the infantry formed hollow squares, three ranks deep, the outer rank kneeling with the butts of their muskets resting on the ground and the bayonets pointing up and outwards. A steady square, which quickly closed whatever gaps were shot in its ranks, could not be taken by cavalry, largely because the horses, having wills of their own, could not be made to charge the hedge of bayonets. A square was also the strongest psychological formation. There was somebody guarding your back, and you could not run away except by running out of the companionship and comparative safety of the square, and into the danger outside it.

Squares were mainly defensive. But cavalry could also be defeated, either by grape or canister shot from artillery, or by other cavalry: a cavalry force which maintained its ranks was always stronger than one which had lost its cohesion under fire.

In a standard attack, the artillery first opened fire, a long-range and more or less indiscriminate bombardment to disorganize the enemy, and the skirmishers also advanced with the same intention. Then the infantry marched forward, holding their fire until the last few paces from the enemy line. They were often accompanied by horse artillery, which stopped to fire and then galloped on again. After firing their muskets, the infantry charged with the bayonet, and there was a crucial moment when the cavalry should arrive— after the front line of the enemy's artillery was overrun, and before his infantry had time to form squares. With that exact timing, the battle was as good as won: the cavalry slashed the enemy line to pieces, and the infantry marched through it. But of course it was seldom so simple. If the enemy infantry held on a little longer than expected, his artillery might still be free to use its grape and canister on the cavalry; and if the cavalry became disorganized, the enemy cavalry, still in its ranks, was also given a moment when it could counter-charge and suddenly turn the tide.

A field commander's first need, especially in defence, was therefore a steady and disciplined infantry, who would maintain their ranks whatever happened. His second need was a sense of tactical timing. And this implied a sense of anticipation, because he had no way of signalling his orders—the only signals given at Waterloo were by officers waving their hats. He had to send his orders, verbally or in writing, by mounted aides-de-camp. At best, they took an appreciable time to deliver them, even within the limits of the battlefield, and at worst they might be unhorsed or wounded or killed on the way, or simply get lost in the mêlée and fail to find the man the orders were addressed to.

All this was common knowledge among the hosts of men. And there was one other thing so deeply imbedded in their consciousness that one must take account of it. This was their reverence for their regimental colours. Standards no doubt began in armies far back in history simply as rallying points, to help soldiers who were lost among the crowds on battlefields. But just as uniforms had evolved from mere utility until they were symbols of masculinity and

The Emperor presents the colours

bravery, so standards evolved to symbolize what men believed they were fighting for. The colours in all armies were presented to the regiments by their Sovereigns in solemn ceremony, and so became precious tokens of patriotism and regimental pride. They were also blessed by priests, and when they were honourably shot to pieces the tattered remains were sewn on to nets and hung up in cathedrals. So they were given a holy significance, too. To lose its standard to the enemy was a disgrace which could haunt a regiment for a whole generation: to defend it, men cast away their lives: to capture an enemy standard was every good soldier's ultimate ambition, the height of his concept of glory.

*　　*　　*

So the morning passed: the Emperor sitting crouched in his farm-house armchair preoccupied, one must assume, with his secret pain, three-quarters of a mile behind his line: the Duke riding here and there in front of his, in the best of health, apparently perfectly calm, seldom talking to anyone and strangely detached in spirit from the men he was leading: and the soldiers in both the armies either bored or clumsily hiding their nervousness, and wondering what they were waiting for, as soldiers so often do. And all of them, from the marshals to the privates, were sharing one assumption: that Napoleon would attack and Wellington would defend. There was quite a long period when Wellington's army was ready and Napoleon's was not. Years afterwards, the Duke in a boastful mood said he would have attacked at Quatre Bras or Waterloo if he had had his Peninsula army, and that the French would not have lasted three minutes. But the army he had was different, and if anyone thought that morning of revers-ing the roles and attacking the French while they were still assembling, nobody spoke of it. Both armies awaited Napoleon's pleasure.

At last, he gave an order—not for an attack in strength on the British line, but for an opening diversion against the outpost in the château of Hougoumont. Far on the left of the French line, artillery opened fire against this target. When the roar of the guns first rolled across the valley, many British officers looked at their watches, but after two days of campaigning most of their watches were wrong. Nobody on either side had been told to keep an official journal of the day, and in the excitement, once the battle was joined, everyone more or less lost count of the passage of time: one man was certain afterwards that the whole thing had only lasted two hours. So nobody knew then, or knows now, exactly what time the Battle of Waterloo began. Probably it was just after half past eleven.

The 52nd Foot, behind the ridge at the back of Hougoumont, was in the line of fire, and the rounds which overshot the château and its buildings came bounding through the rye. Young Ensign Leeke had just been ordered to carry the regimental colours. It was an honour and a responsibility—and besides, as he modestly said, he had not been long enough in the regiment to be of any other use, but this was something he was sure he could do. He stood in the rye field, proudly holding the standard and watching the first of the balls with great respect. 'There, Mr. Leeke, is a cannon shot,' said his sergeant, 'if you never saw one before, sir.'

Gunner of the Foot Artillery of the Garde Impérial

NOON

Attack on Hougoumont—Artillery fire
The infantry attack
The British cavalry charge

NOON

British artillery on the ridge above Hougoumont soon began to reply: and exactly opposite Ensign Leeke, on the other side of the château, another young man stood holding another standard with equal pride, and watching the cannon balls with equal apprehension. His name was Silvain Larreguy de Civrieux, he came from Marseilles, and he could have told a story exactly parallel to Leeke's—the sudden boyish impulse to put on an elegant uniform, join the army and look for adventure and glory, and the loving mother who hugged him and begged him not to go. The greatest difference between them— apart from being on opposite sides in the impending battle—was that Larreguy was a year and a half older than Leeke, and had made his decision when he was only just sixteen. So he had spent three years in the French army, and had already seen bloodthirsty action against the British in Spain. A few days before, on the march towards Waterloo, he had passed his nineteenth birthday, and he looked on himself as a veteran.

Larreguy had reason for feeling apprehensive, in spite of his experience of battle. The artillery fire was doing more damage to his regiment than to Leeke's, because Napoleon's generals had not taken Wellington's precaution of drawing up the troops on sheltered ground. Larreguy was facing the château across a narrow valley which lay to the south-west of it. He could see the richochets coming, curving against the sky, and he had no protection from them. For him and his companions, the battle began with a stern test of courage: to stand and do nothing while men were being blown to pieces right and left of them. They stood there a long time waiting for orders, until Prince Jerome himself, who commanded that wing of the Emperor's line, came riding along it with his staff and observed that they would be safer if they advanced towards the enemy, down the valley slope. Down there, the cannon shot whistled harmlessly over their heads and pitched on the ground they had left. Beyond, on the crest of the farther slope, the grey stone walls of the barns and yard of the château rose like a small fortress. Larreguy saw that the walls had been breached with loopholes: and through the holes, along the foot of the walls, and in woods to the right of them, he saw the red coats of British troops. His regiment waited for the order to join the assault.

Hougoumont

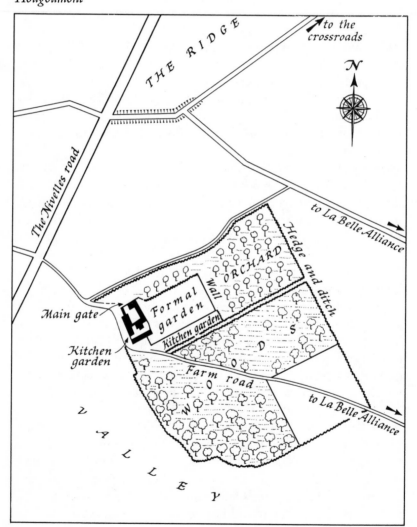

This was no place for a formal advance in line: it must be hand-to-hand fighting among the woods and buildings. So it was no place to hazard the regimental standard. An order came to carry it to the rear and leave it under a guard of sergeant-majors. To Larreguy, that seemed to reflect on his own courage, and he refused to do it. His disobedience earned him a cheer from the regiment, and when the word came to attack, he marched in the van up the slope in front of him.

* * *

Wellington had ridden down to Hougoumont about half an hour before the bombardment began. General Müffling, who went with him, told him he thought the place was untenable—and indeed it was nearer the French lines than the British. 'Ah,' said the Duke, 'but you do not know Macdonell.' And he pointed to the Scottish colonel who commanded the garrison.

James Macdonell was a reassuringly massive Highlander, the son of centuries of feuds between rival clans, and he had light companies of the Scots Guards and Coldstream Guards in his isolated command. The importance of his outpost was the narrow valley which the château overlooked. It was invisible from the main position, and it was deep enough, as Larreguy and his regiment had discovered, to offer protection from the British artillery on the ridge. It started not far from La Belle Alliance, and led across the high road from Nivelles. If it was left unguarded, the French could move in safety round the flank of Wellington's position. The ridge, without the château, was indefensible, and that fact had been as obvious to Napoleon as it had to Wellington.

In spite of what Müffling said, the château and its grounds were not an intrinsically weak position. The house itself was connected to a range of buildings, granaries, cowsheds, barns and two lesser houses, the farmer's and the gardener's; and the whole range surrounded two yards which were divided by a chapel and a low wall with a gate in it. Behind the main house to the east, the side which faced La Haye Sainte, there was a large formal garden enclosed by a six-foot wall. Beyond that, there was an orchard, and to the south, towards the French position, a thickly planted wood. The Guards occupied the buildings, the garden and the orchard. The wood was held by Germans.

The south side of Hougoumont in 1815 . . .

Macdonell and his men, unlike the rest of the army, had spent a busy night. They had fortified the place by making loopholes, building firing platforms, and blocking all the gates to the yard enclosed by the buildings, with the exception of the main gate on the northern side, which they kept open for supplies and communication. But the men at work in the buildings had been better off than those who were out in the orchard and the woods, for those advanced posts were in contact with the French all night, and the men in them were not only wet to the skin but were kept in a state of alert.

*   *   *

The defence of Hougoumont suffered afterwards, even more than the main part of the battle, from romantic and heroic story-telling. It certainly was a heroic feat of arms. But the stories were written in admiration by people who were not there. Very few of the men who were there told their stories at all, and those who did told more about the minor discomforts of the day than about its heroic episodes.

. . . and today

Perhaps this reflected a traditional attitude of mind in the highly professional soldiers of the Guards: to be wet was unpleasant, to be dirty was unsoldierly, but to be heroic was expected of a guardsman, and therefore was undignified to mention. The same attitude was said to be seen in the British cavalry. They were nothing if not heroic, but Mercer observed that troopers who fell off their horses at Quatre Bras and got their breeches muddy were sent off the field as being unfit to appear on parade.

Out in the orchard was a young and humble guardsman called Private Matthew Clay. He had some excuse for remembering the discomfort more clearly than the battle, because of all the wet men on the field that morning, he was among the wettest. His battalion had fought at Quatre Bras on Friday, and retreated all day on Saturday; and on Saturday evening, in the thunderstorm, it halted in a field of clover near Hougoumont and was ordered to pitch its blankets.

This was a process known only to the Guards. Every man in the army carried one blanket, but the Guards' blankets were provided with a button-hole and a tape in each corner. To pitch blankets, men were numbered in fours, and each four drew lots to decide upon two whose blankets should be pitched. The unlucky two stood their muskets upright on the ground, put the knobs of the ramrods through the holes in two corners of the blankets, and pegged out the other corners to make a very primitive ridge tent. (It was in one such tent that Gronow had his champagne breakfast.) Private Clay was unlucky in the draw. He and his three companions crawled into their tent with all the rest of their equipment, expecting to spend the night there. But they had only been in it long enough for the blankets to be soaked when they were told to move, and to man the hedges of the orchard. It took Clay a long time—it was dark by then—to stow the sodden blanket into his knapsack again. By the time he had finished, the battalion had vanished and left him alone in the field. In trying to follow it, he fell into a ditch which was full of water up to his neck. And then he shivered in the hedge all night, peering through it at the French who were in a field of corn on the other side. At dawn, he was allowed to light a fire, and one man of his company found and killed a pig. Clay's portion was part of its head. He put it on the fire, and when it was warm and covered with soot he tried to eat it. He had had nothing to eat for thirty-six hours, but it was too disgusting. He put the remains of it into his knapsack, with the wet blanket and all his other possessions, and turned to his soldierly duty: to clean his musket, ready for the day.

Hougoumont was defended by a few hundred men like Clay: wet, hungry, miserable, tired and dumbly heroic. Nobody told them exactly why they had to defend that particular Belgian farmyard to the death. They were simply told to do it, so they did.

When the bombardment started, the first thing Private Clay was told to do was to leave the orchard where he had watched all night, and move with his company round the northern side of the buildings and down a lane which ran between the wall of the barn and the valley. On that side of the farm, he found a long narrow vegetable garden, enclosed by another hedge. His company lined the hedge, kneeling behind it. There, they were face to face with Larreguy's regiment: its skirmishers were coming through the corn along the valley bottom. He tried to pick them out through the branches. From the loopholes in the wall behind him, other guardsmen opened a rapid fire of musketry over his head. To his left, in the wood, there were sounds of furious fighting. Down there, the French were bringing up guns, and grape shot began to plough through the garden behind him. It was uncomfortable. By squeezing into the hedge, he could keep his body out of the blast of shot, but stray missiles, richochets perhaps, kept hitting his knapsack and the heels of his shoes. It seemed a long time they stayed in that position. The shouting and musketry in the wood were coming closer, the French were advancing through it, the hedge seemed likely to be taken from the rear. Clay was glad when the word was passed along to go back by the way they had come, and retreat inside the farmyard. It was none too soon, he thought.

But at Hougoumont a good many orders were disobeyed: the formal movements of infantry training were impossible there, every man had to fight like a skirmisher. So young officers and even private soldiers made decisions of their own. But on both sides the disobedience, like Larreguy's, was in being more belligerent, in taking more risks, not less. Now a lieutenant down in the hedge near Clay decided to disobey the order to retreat, and stood up with his sword in one hand and his cap in the other and shouted for volunteers to advance. Clay was caught up in the group of men who joined him, and while the company marched for the gate of the farmyard, they ran in the opposite direction, towards the wood.

Clay never knew what happened to the rest. He came to a large round haystack and stood behind it, biting off cartridges, loading, ramming and firing as fast as he could at glimpses of Frenchmen close to him in the corn and among the trees. His musket kept misfiring: its wood had swollen in the wet of the night and jammed the spring of the firelock. Worrying over that, and the shots that were coming at him, he did not see if the others retreated or were killed. He suddenly found they had gone, and he and one other man were alone outside the farmyard.

*   *   *

Clay at that stage was so preoccupied with his musketry that he was hardly aware of the slaughter going on all round him. Silvain Larreguy, however, advanced into it, half an hour perhaps after the fighting started, and he saw it with fresh eyes. In the wood, along the wall of the garden and round the farmyard itself, huge numbers

Defence of the main gate of Hougoumont

of French, the whole of an infantry division, had already marched into the fire of the Germans and British hidden behind the walls and among the trees. Larreguy retained a dreadful impression of being splashed with blood, of his own feet being wet with it as if he had waded in it, and of expecting second by second to be killed or horribly wounded. But he also remembered the exaltation of it: how the wounded refused to leave the field, how the dying called down blessings on the Emperor, how his own captain, shot through by two musket-balls, kept urging them on in a voice that grew weaker until he fell.

*   *   *

Inside the farmyard and the walled flower garden, there was not much need for officers to issue any orders. The French were surging round outside, the need to keep them out was plain and simple. Every man at every loophole and window had targets in front of him every time he could load. The officers dismounted, sheathed their swords and took the muskets of the dead. The wounded crawled into the barns, the cowsheds, the chapel and the kitchens. But before anyone knew it or expected it, the French were right

The chapel and courtyard today

round at the back of the buildings. Hidden by gunsmoke, they came round the orchard and the garden and rushed the main gate of the yard. The gate was still open. A few men outside it were taken by surprise and put up a bloodthirsty fight. The French general in command was killed there, and his colonel was unhorsed by a Scottish sergeant, who seized the horse and rode it into the court-yard. The defenders fell back fighting through the gateway. About a hundred Frenchmen followed them in.

Colonel Macdonell was in the garden when he heard the trium-phant shouts of the French behind him. He rushed back into the yard. Men were fighting hand to hand all over it with axes, musket butts and swords. Some Guards had retreated up the steps to the doorway of the château, some were firing down at the mob from the château windows. Three of his officers and a sergeant heard him shout and followed him across to the gateway, scattering everyone: the five of them put their shoulders to the gates. Frenchmen pressed in from outside, but they had no reinforcements. Macdonell forced the gates back until they shut and the sergeant dropped the massive bar of wood which locked them. 'The success of the battle of Waterloo depended on the closing of the gates': so Wellington wrote afterwards. It had been a near thing. They heaped up flag-stones, broken carts and firewood against them. And inside the yard they hunted the Frenchmen down, until the only one alive and unhurt was a drummer boy, unarmed, who had lost his drum.

But Private Clay, a man of little importance except to himself, was still outside the fortress. The gates were shut when he reached them, and all his friends had gone. He stood with his back to the wall of the barn, conspicuous in his red coat, and he could see the French snipers aiming at him and hear the near misses smacking the stones beside him. Another musket caught his eye. He threw his own away and picked it up. It was warm from use, and he was comforted to find the spring was working.

*   *   *

The fight at Hougoumont raged for an hour and a half before any-thing else happened on the battlefield, except that the cannon shot which missed the château still came bouncing through the ranks of waiting men and picked off a victim here and there. Sergeant Wheeler, with an old soldier's luck, was posted in the sunken lane far on the right where the road to Nivelles crossed it by a bridge, and from that safe billet he watched the shot going over. Ensign Leeke saw plenty of them, both shot and shell, because he was just behind Hougoumont. To escape the worst of the danger, his regi-ment had been told to lie down, and he had his head on the knapsack of his kind and fatherly sergeant. A piece of shell the size of the palm of his hand went through the sergeant's mess tins with a sudden rattle and stuck in one of them. 'If that had hit either you or me on the head, sir,' said the sergeant, 'I think it would have settled our business for us.' And Leeke felt more proud than alarmed at the narrow escape. But then he saw two men of the regiment lying dead under a tree, the first men he had ever seen killed in a battle, and he had to try hard not to cry at the melancholy sight.

Captain Mercer, when the cannonade began, was still digging potatoes in the garden of La Haye Sainte, and his troop of artillery was still in the orchard below the farmhouse. At first, he did not take much notice of the noise, but at last he looked out of the garden to see what was happening, and was astonished to find that all the bivouacs on the slope of the valley were deserted. The ground that

raising stories of Quatre Bras, where each of Picton's regiments had lost over a third of its men: the Gordons, they said, had lost more, half their number and twenty-five of their thirty-six officers. So now, they were thin on the ground. They covered a length of the line which should have been defended by a whole division, and when they were formed two deep there was nobody left in reserve. But none of them seemed dismayed: they watched the French preparations with a soldier's unimaginative interest, content to be spectators.

But Kincaid thought the bottom of the valley in the front of him looked suspiciously innocent. There was nobody in it. And then he saw innumerable black specks approaching in the distance and taking post at regular intervals. They were cannon: symptoms, he thought, that they were not to be spectators very long.

*　　　*　　　*

There were seventy-four of the cannon, in fact, and they were assembled by Marshal Ney on a minor spur of slightly rising ground which projected into the valley below La Belle Alliance. Behind them, still largely out of sight from the British side, he had 17,000 infantry men in columns. And just before one o'clock, he sent word back to Napoleon that everything was ready.

Marshal Ney was down in the valley, and he stayed there all day. But the Emperor was still on the knoll beside the road at Rossomme, still sitting in the farm armchair absorbed in his own thoughts. Once in a while, his staff saw him suddenly start to his feet and sweep the horizon with his telescope. From his position he could see across to the wood of Hougoumont, and to the top of the ridge in the distance that Wellington was defending. But the ground in front of him hid the bottom of the valley, and he could not see for himself what was happening down there.

When the aide brought the message from Ney, Napoleon rose to his feet again and took a final look through the telescope at the parts of the field of battle he could see; it went without saying that when his huge battery of guns began to fire, most of the view would be hidden by the smoke. And far to his right, on the edge of a wood five miles away, he saw some troops. All his staff trained their telescopes on the spot. Some thought it was only bushes or the shadow of a cloud. Some said they could distinguish Prussian uniforms, others that they were French. They were not left long to

Napoleon at Rossomme

argue. A captured officer of cavalry was brought in. He was Prussian, and he said the troops were the advance guard of one of Marshal Blücher's corps, on its way to join Wellington.

Here was proof of Jerome's piece of gossip, which Napoleon had dismissed as impossible nonsense. But he did not seem perturbed. 'This morning we had ninety odds in our favour,' he said. 'We still have sixty against forty.' He had just dictated a letter to Marshal Grouchy, confirming in an indecisive manner that he should continue to advance towards the village of Wavre, where the Prussians had last been reported. Now at last, in a postscript, he added a definite order: 'Do not lose a minute to draw nearer to us and join us.' But Grouchy was fifteen miles away, as the crow flies, and more by the lanes. A mounted officer took two and a half hours to cover the distance, and Grouchy's thousands of men, on foot and with their guns and wagons, would have taken much longer. He could not have arrived in time to join the battle before the night put a stop to it.

Napoleon ordered cavalry out to intercept the Prussians, and infantry to support them. But he made no change in the plan he had set his mind on, a direct attack in the classical manner to destroy the army of Wellington. And at half past one, the seventy-four guns in front of La Belle Alliance simultaneously opened fire.

*   *   *

Wellington's veterans had never known such a heavy cannonade: afterwards, looking back on the day, survivors remembered the artillery fire as much the hardest thing they had to bear. The stray shots from Hougoumont had only been the mildest preparation: now the great iron balls, eight and twelve pounders, came thickly bounding up and over the ridge, each carving an instant bloody channel through the ranks. The power of artillery at such a range was not in the number of men it killed but in the horrible way it did it. Cannon balls did not wound: they smashed a man to pieces. Sergeant Lawrence, in the rear of his regiment, saw a shell cut his sergeant-major in half and take off the head of a grenadier he knew: and then as it flew past him it exploded and blew him off his feet. He picked himself up, little hurt: the handle of his sword was turned black, he noticed, and the tail of his sash was burnt off. As an old soldier, he could put on an air of sang-froid. 'Sharp work to begin with, I hope it will end better,' he said to a fellow sergeant. But a young recruit close by called out to him in distress, saying he was taken ill and must fall out of rank. Lawrence pushed him back into his place. 'Why, it's the smell of this little powder that has caused your illness,' he said. 'There's nothing else the matter with you.' But the boy fell down and would not move. Cowardice, Lawrence thought: he ought to be shot.

This was what artillery was meant to do, to destroy the courage of the enemy before the attack began. Napoleon's massive battery might have been expected to succeed. But two things held Wellington's army together in that preliminary test. One was the toughness of men like Lawrence: the other was the Duke's own foresight in assembling most of the army behind the ridge. The ridge was slightly higher than the guns. The shots which hit the top of it came bouncing over, but those which passed over it went on quite a long way before they fell. Consequently, there was a narrow zone of comparative safety just behind it. During the ordeal, the Duke ordered part of his front line to withdraw behind the crest, and most of the regimental commanders told their men to lie down. To the French officers who were watching from the other side of the valley, most of the British line appeared to vanish, and they hoped it had broken and fled.

But one brigade had been left on the forward slope, as if to prove by its fate the wisdom of the rest of the Duke's dispositions. This was the brigade of Belgian infantry that Corporal Dickson had admired when it took its position on the left of the line, beyond Sir Thomas Picton's Scottish regiments. Everybody else was either under cover or behind the lane and its hedges. The Scottish line had been withdrawn a hundred yards. But the Belgians were on the open sloping field in front of the hedges, in full view of the French and without the slightest protection or support. Nobody ever explained why they were left there, or why the Duke or Picton did not tell them to come back. They were no use where they were, and they were exposed to the fire of any French artillery man who cared to train his gun in their direction. So they suffered far more than anybody else, and before the bombardment ended their nerves were at breaking point.

*　　　*　　　*

The worst of it for everyone—as Silvain Larreguy had found—was having nothing to do. You could not hit back. But just as the barrage began, Tom Morris the opinionated Cockney sergeant found a useful occupation. The artillery was already taking off a good many of his men when he saw a commissariat wagon driving on to the field from the Brussels road. He was sent to draw the ration of gin for his company. He had to wait his turn, and he was still there when a shot went through the barrel of gin and the man who was measuring it out. But Morris had his share. In fact, he had more: with soldierly foresight, he had drawn the rations of all the men in his company who were out of action, sick or detached or dead. So when he had shared out the ration to all the men who were present, he still had three full canteens. He had a crony called Sergeant Burton. The two

of them took an extra drop together. Burton told him to keep what
was still left so that they could finish it after the battle. Morris
thought they might be dead by then. 'Tom', Burton said, 'I'll tell
you what it is: there is no shot made yet for either you or me.' The
discussion ended because the regiment had been ordered to lie down,
so Morris lay down too; and he fell fast asleep.

*   *   *

The barrage lasted half an hour, and then it stopped: and in the
sudden silence, Morris was perhaps the only living man who did not
raise his head to listen. And all of them, with their ears still ringing
from the gunfire, heard a new sound in the bottom of the valley out
of sight: cheering, shouting, drums, and soon distinctly the words
they were all to learn before the day was out: *Vive l'Empereur!* The
drums were beating a distinctive rhythm. Old soldiers from Spain
remembered it well, and told the young ones what it was: the *pas de
charge*. Leeke never forgot it, or forgot the moment when he heard
it coming: 'the rum dum, the rum dum, the rummadum dumma-
dum, dum, dum'. Gronow heard it: a sound, he said in a characteristic
understatement, which few men, however brave they might be,
could listen to without a somewhat unpleasant sensation. Kincaid
heard it too: and he was one of the few who also saw what was
coming, because he had stayed through the whole bombardment on
top of the ridge by the crossroads, in front of the hedges which lined
the lane. In the valley which had been empty, beside the deserted
main road, a huge column of infantry was marching straight towards
him, and on its right and left were other columns, and cavalry on the
flanks. Beyond, the farther side of the valley was a mass of marching
men. He had never seen such a column in battle, and never imagined
it: thousands after thousands, not deployed in battle line but marching
like troops in review, an immense solid block of them that looked
invincible and indestructible, as if its sheer momentum would carry
it irresistibly through the slender line that faced it. Ahead of it, the
officers were brandishing their swords: ahead of them, a line of
skirmishers ran and stopped to fire and ran again. Kincaid's brigade
of riflemen opened fire and brought the skirmishers to a halt, but the
column marched on through them, up the rising slope, past the
orchard of La Haye Sainte and the outpost in the buildings there. The

shouts, the rummadum of drums, the tantara of trumpets, all grew in intensity as it came inexorably nearer. And he and his men watched it coming in total silence.

*   *   *

It looked irresistible, and that was the intention behind it: it was meant to look irresistible. Napoleon's Grand Army had used such massive columns before. They were a psychological formation, and they had smashed their way through defending lines all over Europe simply by their appearance of overwhelming power. But they were not a practical fighting formation. They were vulnerable, and they could be defeated by a stubborn defiance they had seldom met. And the columns marching so splendidly into the valley, for all their superhuman appearance, were beset by trivial human troubles before they were half way across. There was too much shouting, too much

The French Infantry Attack

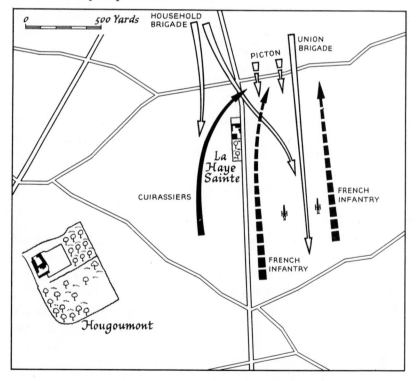

drumming: against those noises and the gunfire, men could not hear their officers' orders. And there was too much mud. As the columns trampled through the rye, the long tough stalks of it tangled round the legs of the men and made them stumble, and caught in the fastenings of their gaiters. One after another, they lost a shoe in the mud and hobbled on with one foot bare, because they could not stop. All of them had huge cakes of mud on their feet which made them clumsy.

Martin, the young Swiss officer, was in the leading column, and he was laughing. In front of him, there was a very tall thin officer he knew. In Spain, this man had made himself a reputation for something less than bravery, and now he seemed to feel his head was unfairly high above everyone else's: he had picked a position close behind a burly soldier and was marching bent double like a question mark. Then, sensing perhaps that men behind him thought his posture was unseemly, he turned round and began to march backwards, balancing his sword on his two hands as officers sometimes did on parade to keep their troops in line. But in order not to lose his shelter, he then bent over backwards. Well, Martin thought, the man had something to boast about at last: he had raised a laugh in a solemn situation.

For between his chuckles Martin was wondering, with his customary independence, why they were advancing in that clumsy and massive formation, and who had ordered it. He could not see anything in its favour. The column was twenty-four ranks deep and about 150 wide. The men in the middle could not see where they were going, or what was happening. Hemmed in by everyone else, their muskets were useless. At best, only the front three ranks could open fire: the rest might almost as well have come empty-handed. It was not even a formation which could quickly change, by any normal drill, into any other: it could not suddenly deploy to increase its fire power, or suddenly form square to defend itself against cavalry. And almost worst of all, it was a sitting target for artillery. A cannon shot which hit a man in the front rank was likely to hit the twenty-three behind him, and down in the valley the shot was coming fast.

*   *   *

The first to confront the advancing columns was the Belgian brigade which had been left on the forward slope of the ridge. What happened to those men was what the French tacticians expected to happen everywhere. They were already strained beyond endurance by the artillery fire. Sir Thomas Picton, who was their divisional commander, was watching from the crest, and he saw them begin to waver. An aide-de-camp said he thought they were going to run. 'Never mind,' Sir Thomas said, 'they shall have a taste of it at any rate.' But they did not even wait for the skirmishers who preceded the columns. Suddenly and simultaneously, as if an order had been given, the whole brigade broke and turned and ran, up the hill and over the hedges and the lane. The desperate men in a torrent swept away their own reserve battalion and a battery of artillery men behind them, and collided here and there with British troops, who hissed and booed and cursed them and had to be restrained from shooting them. Their officers tried to stop the panic flight, but the whole brigade disappeared beyond the ridge towards the forest and was not seen again for the rest of the day. Nobody ought to have blamed them. They had no passionate loyalty, nothing to induce the mad elation they would have needed to try to hold the impossible place that Picton or the Duke had put them in. They left a wide gap in the tenuous line and put the whole of it in added peril. But in their own way they encouraged the men who saw them go: when your own courage is stretched to its limit, it can be strengthened by the sight of someone who seems to have less than you. And what was more, their flight decoyed the French into a position they could not escape from.

Kincaid was too much preoccupied to notice this upheaval a couple of hundred yards to his left. What seemed to be the main column was coming over a little mound in front of him. When the heads of the leading rank showed over it, the Rifles poured a volley into them. Martin, in the ranks behind, was aware of that volley: men fell in front, others tripped over them, the check ran back through all the other ranks, and the column closed up on itself in an even denser mass. But only for a moment: the drums increased their tempo, the leading officers shouted '*En avance!*', men answered with even more triumphant shouts and dragged their muddy boots through the last few paces to the ridge. Kincaid saw the column incline to its right, away from the rifle fire.

Sir Thomas Picton

Martin saw nothing, except the backs of the men in front of him. Only the leaders of the column could see. What they saw was an active body of riflemen to their left, and, to their right, a long stretch of the double hedge on the lane which seemed to be deserted and undefended. They had seen the Belgians run: they could only believe that everyone had run. But the hedges themselves were an obstacle. They were perfectly easy for isolated men to cross, there were plenty of gaps and you could force your way through almost anywhere. But a solid column could not march through them and preserve its close formation while it did so. Forty yards below the hedges the column was therefore halted and ordered to deploy into line, an awkward and prolonged manœuvre in which the rear battalions turned alternately right and left and marched out from behind the leaders.

But the hedges were not deserted. Picton's Scottish infantry had been a hundred yards behind them, sheltering from the gunfire. As the French approached, he ordered his thin and weakened line to advance—two deep, it was the only infantry between the French and Brussels. The timing was fortuitous but perfect. Just as the French began their deployment the Scotsmen reached the hedges: they seemed to Martin to rise up out of the ground. Picton shouted 'Fire!' and at forty paces, 3,000 muskets were discharged across the hedges: the French, with five times the number of men, could hardly bring 500 muskets to bear. Before the roll of the shooting had died away, men could hear Picton shouting 'Charge! Charge! Hurrah!' It was the last thing he said: a bullet hit him in the temple and he fell on the neck of his horse and was dead before they could lift him to the ground. But the men had answered with a shout and burst through the hedges, and the armies were at bayonet point.

Each man's awareness contracted then to the yard or two he could see in the yelling struggling mass, and to the other men within a bayonet's thrust who would kill him unless he killed them. All the British had fired their muskets: they had nothing but bayonets to use. Some of the French were still loaded and fired in the mêlée, as likely to hit a friend as an enemy. Martin remembered crossing the hedges, and hearing his countrymen shouting 'Victoire!' before they were driven back. Each regimental standard, French and British, was the centre of furious fights, men eager for the glory of seizing it, men dying to defend it. The ensign carrying one of the British colours was wounded and fell just after he crossed the hedge. A lieutenant took it and charged on. In front of him, a French officer's horse was shot. The officer jumped up and snatched the staff of the colour, the lieutenant held on to the silk the Frenchman tried to draw his sabre but a sergeant stabbed him with a pike. A British major shouted 'Save the brave fellow!', but it was too late, somebody shot him dead. Kincaid, on the right of the worst of it, was on his horse in a gap in the hedge and saw Sir James Kempt galloping along the line: Kempt had been second-in-command, and Picton's death in the critical moment had thrown the command on him. He called Kincaid by name, and told him never to quit that spot. Kincaid shouted back that he might depend upon it—and immediately found himself unlikely to quit it either alive or dead. For he saw the next field covered with French cuirassiers galloping towards his gap: it was the classic attack, the cavalry coming in to finish what the infantry had started. He put his hand down to draw his sword, determined not to die without a gesture—and the rain of the night had rusted it in the scabbard, and he could not get it out.

But the French were breaking. Paralysed by their formation, caught in the act of their deployment, they could not fight in the way they had been taught. The surprise of the volley had thrown them into confusion, the charge had made it chaos, and chaos could only end in panic. Battalions in front fell back on others half deployed. Units were mixed, men lost their officers and everyone they knew: with nowhere to turn for orders, leaderless flocks of them ran down the hill again. Officers, Martin among them, tried to force men they did not know into orderly ranks again. And at the moment when Martin was pushing a soldier into a rank he was trying to form out of nothing, the man was felled by a sabre and a horse galloped past him. He turned round and for a split second he saw the British cavalry charging, before the horses knocked him over and trampled him down among the dead and wounded. Kincaid saw them too, in the moment of ignominious panic when he could not draw his sword: tens, hundreds, thousands of horses all round him, flowing full gallop over the crossroads, taking the double hedges like steeplechasers, over and through the French who were fleeing on foot, and headlong down the hill and into the ranks of cuirassiers.

*   *   *

Corporal Dickson was back with his regiment, the Scots Greys, when the volley was fired, in his place in the double rank of 300 great grey horses standing so close that the stirrups touched. He saw the Highlanders break through the hedge and vanish down the slope beyond. And he saw his general up there, Sir William Ponsonby, in a fur-trimmed cloak and a great cocked hat, riding a small bay hack —his groom and his charger were lost. The general's aide waved his hat: the colonel shouted 'Scots Greys, charge!' and waved his sword in the air and rode straight at the hedges in front and took them in grand style. 'Now's your chance!' said another penetrating voice: the Duke of Richmond in the thick of things again. Everyone cheered, Dickson gave Rattler the spurs, she reared and sprang forward, neighing and snorting and leapt the hedges, going like the wind— and he had a glimpse of the whole line of proud war-horses dashing along, heads down and flowing manes, tearing up the earth below their hoofs. Crossing the lane they cheered again, 'Scotland for ever!', for down in the din and smoke on the slope before them they could hear the pipers playing and see the feather bonnets of the Highlanders.

Dickson tightened his grip to go down the muddy hill. The Gordons' line was ahead of him, but nothing could check the charge. He heard their officers shouting to them to wheel back by sections, to let the cavalry through, but some of them had no time and were knocked down and ridden over. 'Go at them the Greys!' the Gordons shouted. 'Scotland for ever!' And many tried to grasp the riders' stirrups and run with the horses. Dickson charged full tilt into a belt of smoke where he could not see five yards ahead, and there were the French: wounded men shot at him as he passed, a young officer made a slash at him with his sword but he parried it and broke the man's arm: and then men were throwing down their muskets, crying out for quarter. Through the smoke he saw his sergeant, a giant of a man named Ewart, slashing right and left with the ghastly cold-bloodedness of an expert swordsman at half a dozen men defending their standard. 'One made a thrust at my groin,' Ewart said afterwards, 'I parried it off and cut him down through the head. A lancer came at me—I threw the lance off by my right side and cut him through the chin and upwards through the teeth. Next, a foot-soldier fired at me, and then charged me with his bayonet, which I also had the good luck to parry, and then I cut him down through

Sergeant Ewart seized the standard

the head.' And he seized the standard with its golden eagle of the 45th 'Invincibles', inscribed with the victories of Austerlitz and Jena. General Ponsonby had seen the encounter too. 'My brave fellow, take that to the rear,' he shouted, 'you have done enough till you get rid of it.' And Ewart rode off the field in triumph, while Dickson shouted 'Well done, my boy,' and spurred on across the bottom of the valley in an ecstasy of slaughter, sabring Frenchmen who had no escape, in mud where the horses sank to their knees. And the horses also fought ferociously—Rattler bit and tore at everything in her way.

And then the colonel (also called Ponsonby) galloped past, shouting 'Charge the guns!', and went up the hill towards the battery that had made such havoc half an hour before. Dickson never saw him again, somebody saw him wounded in both arms, still going hell for leather with the reins in his teeth. But everyone had followed him, a mixture by now of all the regiments, to sabre the gunners in revenge, lame the artillery horses and cut their traces and harness. The artillery drivers were only boys, Dickson thought, and they wept aloud as he cut at them. Somebody shouted to him to dismount, that Rattler was badly wounded. He did, and she fell heavily. He caught a French officer's horse and rode on.

*   *   *

Martin lay on the ground pretending to be dead while the cavalry charge went over him, shocked and dazed by the horror of what was happening, waiting for the blow that would kill him. Part of his brain was still working, as it had been trained to work. He ought to get up, he thought: but what could he do by getting up? Nothing but give himself up as a prisoner, or try to cross the valley again among the attackers, which seemed impossible and senseless. But after the thunder of the hoofs had passed, he did get up, and began to try to run. The instinct of freedom, he thought afterwards, must be as strong as love of life.

He stumbled back the way he had come, through the mud and the rye, now trampled and bloody, among the fallen men and horses, dead and dying. It seemed a nightmare: he wanted to run, but the rye-stalks tripped him, he slipped in the mud and blood and he could hardly breathe. British cavalry were riding all about him, sometimes in ranks, sometimes singly, sometimes so close that he flinched from the sabre-cut he expected. To his surprise, they hardly seemed to see him, as if they had something more important to think about and do. When they charged up the hill to the battery, he was limping up it too, and while they slaughtered the gunners he staggered past the guns, and went on and on till he came to a sunken lane beyond the battlefield. There was nobody there, it was quiet, and he fell down and lay there panting, aware for the first time of a bayonet wound in his leg and the pain in his foot which a horse had trodden on.

*   *   *

Martin underrated the British cavalry. For all the bloodlust that the charge aroused in them, their code of war would not allow them deliberately to kill a wounded man. Dishevelled, muddy, limping and disarmed, the only things he really had to fear were being shot or trampled down again by accident, or rounded up among the herds of prisoners.

The cavalry's exaltation began to fade, solely because their horses were blown and exhausted. Dickson began to think it was time to get away. But looking back towards the distant British line, he now saw regiments of French cuirassiers and lancers galloping across the bottom of the valley. With a professional eye, he admired the sparkling breastplates, the brass helmets, the strong black horses with great blue rugs across the croups. But above him, over the crest of the French ridge, masses of infantry with tall fur hats were coming at the double. All his officers had vanished: half a dozen Greys and a dozen Royals and Inniskillings were all he could see. Somebody shouted 'Come on lads, that's the road home!' and they charged at the lancers. The crash when they met was terrible. He saw the lances rise and fall for a moment, and a friend of his went down. The horses began to rear and bite and kick, and man after man went down among their feet and he saw them trying to ward off the lances with their hands. And then the horse he had taken was killed by a thrust of a lance and he was down himself and thought he was done for, and lay there under the hoofs and heard the clash of arms, the shouting of men, the neighing and moaning of the horses.

And then it passed, and standing up he saw General Ponsonby lying beside his little bay hack, both dead. The general's fur-edged cloak had blown aside, and he saw by his hand a miniature of a lady and his watch. And other officers he knew, his brigade major, a lieutenant, all dead. A cheer brought him back to his senses, and a squadron of British dragoons rode past, pursuing the lancers. And that was the last thing Dickson remembered until he found himself lying with the remnants of his regiment far behind the line where they had started. Of the 300, scarcely fifty had returned. He did not know how he had come there. Somebody told him he had caught a third horse, so wounded that she fell down dead as he was mounting her. But Rattler had come back before him, and was standing there bleeding and riderless in line.

*   *   *

Inniskilling Dragoons

In the middle of all the archaic splendour of the sabre charge, one passionate enthusiast saw his opportunity. His name was Whinyates, he was a major of artillery, and his passion was for rockets. It grieved him that almost everyone else in the army thought rockets were funny. The Duke was scornful about them, and had ordered that Whinyates' troop should leave them behind and use ordinary guns. Somebody had said that would break Whinyates' heart. 'Damn his heart, sir,' the Duke had replied, 'let my order be obeyed.' But for once, it was not. Whinyates had somehow managed to smuggle his apparatus on to the battlefield. He was there behind the lane when the cavalry went through, and he galloped after them with his troop of mounted rocketeers.

There were two ways of firing rockets, either up in the air or along the ground. Up in the air, with luck, they could carry over a mile, but that method needed a cumbersome carriage called a bombarding frame. Whinyates had one, but it was too heavy to take across the lane, so he left it. The n.c.o. in charge of it let fly in the direction of the French lines, and his rockets were seen far and wide before someone grew nervous and told him to stop. But Whinyates rode down to the bottom of the valley and dismounted his men, some-where to the left of the main road, in rye that had not yet been trampled down. They carried rocket sticks in buckets or quivers, six-pound rockets in their holsters, and small iron triangles for horizontal fire. The rye was so high they could not see over it, but they laid the rockets down and fired them through it.

Ground rockets were exciting for friend and foe. You could point them in the right direction, but where they went after that depended upon what they hit as they whizzed along. They had been known to reach a specific target—a few had been fired in the retreat from Quatre Bras, and one had put a gun out of action. But sometimes they shot straight up in the air, and sometimes they turned right round and pursued the men who had fired them. Whinyates himself admitted they should not be fired singly, when their erratic course was only too obvious: but a salvo, he believed, had an imposing appearance.

Poor Whinyates: he was always having to defend his rockets, not from the enemy but from his friends. Perhaps it was a pity he let them off in the middle of a cavalry charge, for the cavalry were the most conservative of soldiers. The charge was their moment of glory, and he might have known they would not want it marred by newfangled devices. Ever afterwards, he had to listen to cavalry officers who grumbled that the rockets had been a nuisance. He was an honest man, he had not been able to see through the rye, and he could not answer them with any claim of success. It was twenty years later before he found one crumb of comfort: someone told him a wounded cavalry major, lying near the French lines, had heard the rockets passing and had heard men cursing them, in French.

*   *   *

At the same moment when the Union Brigade charged over the hedges, the Household Brigade came over the sunken lane on the

The cavalry charge: the Duke on the left,

and Lord Uxbridge on the right

other side of the main road, some charging down the slope to the right of La Haye Sainte against the advancing cuirassiers, and others diagonally over the crossroads against the infantry column. And out in front of them, first of all, was Lord Uxbridge.

He had been far over on the right, directing minor cavalry operations at Hougoumont, when the French attack on the left began to develop; and he galloped back, saw the attacking columns, summed up the situation at a glance, and gave the two brigade commanders hurried shouted orders. And having ordered a massive cavalry charge, it was more than he could resist to put himself at the head of it. But that instant spirited decision was to haunt him all his life. For he soon saw his six regiments were out of hand, galloping on too far, into positions they could not hope to retreat from. Two of them, the Scots Greys and the Blues, should have been in support—those were the orders he had shouted—to cover the retirement of the other four: and he should have been with them, to see that they did it. But up in front, right in the thick of the sabre work, it was out of his power to call a halt: nobody heard his shouts, or the bugle calls he ordered. It was his fate to watch the finest of his cavalry, the finest perhaps the world had ever seen, achieve its triumph and then, intoxicated by its own success, ride on to its own destruction. He rode back chastened, knowing perhaps that what had been achieved would always be celebrated in stories of military glory, but knowing certainly that most of the two brigades would never ride back at all. By the crossroads he met the bevy of diplomatic attachés who surrounded the Duke. 'I never saw so joyous a group,' he wrote afterwards. 'They thought the battle was over.'[1]

And indeed the valley was empty again. But now, several thousand bodies were lying in the mud, dead men, dead horses, wounded men without any hope of help, some riderless horses struggling in their pain, some charging about in fear, and some calmly cropping whatever grass they could find. It looked as if a major battle had been fought and finished. But it had only begun.

---

[1] A story spread in France that the British cavalry was drunk. This is thought to have started because *gris* can mean drunk or grey: so the Scots Greys became *Ecossais gris*.

AFTERNOON

Hougoumont holds out—The Emperor and Marshal Ney
Attack on La Haye Sainte
The cavalry attacks

AFTERNOON

Distance played tricks with the sound of the cannonade. Forces that Wellington had left at the villages of Hal and Tubize, ten miles to the west, did not hear it at all, but 135 miles away in the same direction people heard it on the coast of Kent, or thought they did: on Tuesday, before any news of the battle reached England, the *Kentish Gazette* reported: 'A heavy and incessant firing was heard from this coast on Sunday evening in the direction of Dunkirk.' Marshal Grouchy, fifteen miles to the east, heard it while he was eating strawberries for lunch. Some of his staff urged him to march towards the guns, but he refused because his last orders from the Emperor had been to pursue the Prussians—a decision for which he was criticized ever after. In Brussels the doors and windows shook, and many of the English gentry who still remained there decided the time had come to retreat to Antwerp. But in Antwerp people heard it too: Magdalene De Lancey shut her windows to try to keep it out.

She had made up her mind merely to exist, and not to think, until her husband could come back to her. He had warned her not to listen to rumours, and she had found a room at the back of an inn called Le Grand Laboureur, so shut in by buildings that she could not see or hear the commotion that was going on in the streets of the city. There she stayed, and refused to go out at all, in case a message came from him. But she had a maid named Emma, and on Saturday, the day after Quatre Bras, Emma could not resist standing out in the street, listening to every terrible story that was told of the fighting, and watching wounded men brought in, and carriages full of women and children flying from Brussels. Towards evening, she came in and told her mistress that all the ladies were hastening to England, for the French had taken Brussels. 'Well, Emma,' Lady De Lancey said, 'you know that if the French were firing at this house, I would not move till I was ordered: but you have no such duty, therefore go if you like. I dare say any of the families will let you join them.' And Emma declared she would never leave her, even if she had to go to a French prison.

A captain in Sir William's department brought her what little reliable news there was, and on Saturday night, to her joy, he also brought a letter her husband had written after Quatre Bras. He was safe, and in great spirits: they had given the French a beating. She wrote to him every day, but afterwards she found that none of her letters had reached him.

On Sunday, the captain came to tell her the final effort was to be made that day. All day, she was restless and unhappy, uneasy at the length of their separation. Three days already: she had naïvely expected it all to be over sooner. She was anxious mainly for the outcome of the battle. She never thought her own husband might be hurt; and most of the women, she believed, who were waiting in Antwerp or in Brussels, had the same feeling of their own man's safety, as if love could take care of him whatever happened. And all the afternoon, the distant rumble went on, even with the windows shut against it, scarcely audible and yet pervasive.

*   *   *

Marshal Blücher and his Prussians heard it too, as they struggled along the lanes from the village of Wavre to fulfil the promise he had given Wellington. The sound put an end to the suspicion General Gneisenau had expressed, that Wellington might only intend to make a demonstration.

Blücher's forthright promise and Gneisenau's suspicion had been typical of the marshal and his chief of staff. Blücher was much the most homely of the three commanders who converged on Waterloo that day. Napoleon maintained his dignity behind a screen of pomp: Wellington guarded himself by detachment and inaccessibility. But Blücher was bluff and jolly, and could even, unlike the others, enjoy a joke against himself. As a young officer, he had been so wild and gay that he had been passed over for promotion and had offered his resignation: 'Capt. Blücher can take himself to the devil,' his Emperor had written on it, and from the age of thirty to the age of forty-five he had become a farmer. At seventy-two, he was still

Marshal Blücher

as wild and gay as his age allowed him to be. It endeared him to his troops. He had an engaging habit of calling them 'My children', and they responded by calling him Father Blücher. 'Brave comrades in arms,' he shouted to a Russian contingent after one of his victories, 'I shall thank your Emperor for giving me the honour of command-ing such excellent men.' This friendliness towards the common soldiers was an eccentricity that only a commander old in years could have allowed himself, but it was extremely successful: the Prussians had a human affection for their commander-in-chief that neither the British nor the French enjoyed. And since Blücher had also unbounded energy and courage and a very shrewd sense of strategy and tactics, his armies had always been powerful.

Among his equals, he could seem disarmingly modest, and was always disarmingly trusting. He kept his own promises, and took it for granted that everyone else would keep theirs. He had no great intellect, and cheerfully admitted he had not. At formal parties, he was inclined to entertain or embarrass the guests by making up childish riddles, and he was vastly amused when the University of Oxford offered him an honorary doctorate of law. 'If they make me a doctor,' he said, 'they'll have to make Gneisenau an apothecary. He's the man who administers the pills I prescribe.' It was hard to be sure if he knew there was more than one kind of doctor.

Gneisenau in fact, as his chief of staff, was just the counterbalance he needed: dour, efficient and chronically suspicious, he was always at hand to examine and criticize the promises the marshal gave and accepted so heartily. Wellington's promise had been a case in point. Did Wellington really mean to stand at Waterloo? Was he able to do so? If he found himself in difficulties, would he not put British interests first, pull out and leave the Prussians in a fatal situation? It was said that Gneisenau and Blücher had had an angry argument. Blücher did not always overrule his chief of staff, but he had done so then; and the sound of the massive cannonade proved that this time his trust had been well placed.

Bruised by the fall from his horse at Ligny, and still suffering from the shock of it, he marched with his army all the morning, urging them on when their guns and transport bogged down in the muddy lanes. When he made his promise, he had not reckoned with such lanes. After the night of rain, the main roads that the British and French had used were bad enough: the Prussians were trying to use the cross-lanes, which at their best were only built to carry farm traffic from one village to another. The Prussian troops the Emperor had seen in the middle of the morning were only a vanguard. By the middle of the afternoon, a Prussian force was in action against the French in the village of Plancenoit, to the east of Rossomme. But the main body was still filtering slowly, one wagon at a time, through waterlogged valleys out of sight of the battlefield. Wellington did not know where they were, or whether they would really come in time to fight before the day was over. He only knew that Blücher had promised a thing it was supposed no army could ever do: to fight a major victory before it had recovered from a serious defeat.

*   *   *

There was a pause in the battle. After the rout of the French infantry and the destruction of so much of the British cavalry, both sides needed time to recover and reorganize themselves. It was about three o'clock. Nothing happened for half an hour, except that the artillery started to blaze away again. All along the ridge, men who were not too preoccupied with their own affairs looked towards Hougoumont, for above the grey gunpowder smoke which lay over the field, a great column of black smoke was rising from the château and its farm. And down there, Private Matthew Clay of the Guards, who had found himself alone and shut out of the farm-yard when everyone else was inside, was now in another predicament: on the top floor of the château, which was blazing underneath him.

His escape from the first of these alarming situations showed again how hard it was to hit a target with a musket. While he stood alone in his red coat against the outer wall of the barn, all the French skirmishers could see him from the corn on the other side of the narrow kitchen garden. Being a musketeer himself, he was more bewildered than frightened. A great many of them took a shot at him. But none of them gave him a scratch, and after loading and firing a few rather aimless shots in reply, he saw a small door in the wall and ran for it. It opened, and he went through into the barn, and from that to the courtyard. The first man he recognized there was Colonel Macdonell himself, with blood on his face, carrying what seemed to be a tree-trunk in his arms to reinforce the barricade

The shells set the roofs of Hougoumont on fire

on the main gate. At once, Clay was rounded up with a few other men by an officer who hustled them up to the attics of the château. That was the highest of the buildings, and they began to annoy the French with musketry from the windows.

In war, people often like to believe that what they have done has provoked their enemy to costly retaliation. Clay believed it was his musket-fire from the attic windows that made the French start shelling the château with heavy howitzers. There was this much truth in it: that the stubbornness of all the men like Clay forced the French to go on to the next conventional process of a siege. The howitzer shells set the thatched roofs of the barn and outhouses on fire, and the blaze caught the lower floors of the château itself and spread upwards. The men at the top made a rush for the staircase, but the officer stood at the door and made them stay and keep up their fusillade until the floor was about to collapse. They were hardly out of the place when the roof fell in and a sheet of flame and sparks flew up from it.

To set a building on fire could be expected to force a surrender. At Hougoumont, on the contrary, it may have helped the defence, because the place was built round a courtyard, and the burning buildings made a barrier the French could not hope to penetrate. But it added horror to the suffering of the defenders. The wounded had been put in the buildings, or crawled into them, for shelter. By now, too few were left in action to bring them out again. The survivors had to fight on although most of them knew their friends were being burned alive. Officers' horses stampeded out of the blazing stables, but then ran in again and perished. Men could be seen crawling out with their clothes on fire. The sergeant who had helped to close the gates asked Macdonell for permission to leave his post for a moment, and ran into the barn and dragged his brother out. But most were left to die.

In the next hour or so, Clay came under the orders of three or four different officers: each sent him to a place where a breach was threatening—the main gate, now splintered by round-shot, a shell-hole in the wall above it, a gutted window. He was so intent on defending these places and watching the French who were prowling round outside that he hardly knew of the horrors behind him before the fight was over. Sometimes, he knew, the whole place was sur-rounded and the French were battering again at the gate on the northern side. Sometimes they receded, and reinforcements and

ammunition came down from the ridge. And all the time, the air in
the yard was suffocating: everyone was black with soot and scorched
by flying embers. But the Guards held on. It was not a matter of
organization, but simply of plugging every gap as soon as it was
made. It did not need tactical skill, but it did need perfect fidelity
from every soldier there—a few hundred Clays, so trained that
whatever happened they never thought of surrender or retreat. And
during the afternoon, the attack very slowly began to slacken.

Hougoumont never fell. But oddly enough, Silvain Larreguy,
who carried his regiment's standard there all day, believed it did.
And Captain Robinaux, who also fought in the wood and was a
much more experienced soldier, went even further: as he remembered it afterwards, the French took the château within half an hour
of the start of their attack and held it all day. It may be possible that
both these men, the old soldier and the young volunteer, retreated
into the wood, out of sight of the buildings, after the first attack, and
did not see or even hear that the defence was still alive. Or if they
saw the fire, they may have assumed that nobody could still be
fighting inside it. Or possibly, at the end of a day which brought
disaster to the Emperor's army, the men who attacked the château
persuaded themselves that their part in the battle, at least, had not
been an utter failure. In the shock and shame of defeat, men clung
to beliefs which could save a little of their martial pride. But the
Emperor's senior officers knew the truth: that the Hougoumont
valley remained under British control, and that the advance along it,
which could have outflanked the ridge, remained impossible.

*   *   *

On the ridge, in the lull which followed the British cavalry charge,
the Duke moved his front line infantry back again for shelter from
the artillery bombardment, and everyone lay down, unless he had
something to do. Some reinforcements were moved to the left of
the crossroads; but there was more movement away from the front
line than towards it. Masses of prisoners had been taken—some
people said two thousand, some said four—and they were being
escorted back to the forest and down the road to Brussels. Wounded
men were being helped or carried off the field towards the farm and

the cottages of Mont St. Jean, where the surgeons had set up their posts and were busy already. Naturally, it was a popular job to help a wounded comrade back to safety, and to linger a while before going back to the fight. There was a good chance nobody would stop you if you wore a compassionate expression—especially if you had an officer to carry. But there were no stretchers, and it took six men to carry a wounded man in a blanket. So the loss of manpower through this humane activity could be enormous. Before the battle, some commanders had therefore ordered that nobody was to be helped or carried off, not even themselves, and several who had given that order were left to die where they fell.

And men were deserting. 'I was told it was very ridiculous,' Kincaid wrote afterwards, 'to see the number of vacant spots that were left nearly along the whole of the line, where a great part of the dark-dressed foreign troops had stood.' This was an exaggeration, so early in the day: the British exaggerated the desertions of the Belgians, Dutch and Germans, to enhance their own claims of courage and victory. But one brigade had certainly gone as a whole, and probably parts of others by then had put themselves out of harm's way on one pretext or another: and worse was to happen later. An officer of De Lancey's staff, who rode into the outskirts of the forest while the battle was at its height, saw whole battalions who had piled their arms and were sitting peacefully smoking round camp fires. But it was General Müffling, not the British, who estimated that 10,000 men ran away in the course of the day: and nobody denied it.

Everybody in the front line or near it saw the Duke from time to time as he rode along the ridge, and everybody remarked that he looked calm. He seemed to notice everything that happened, his orders were prompt and exact, and he could always be found when he was needed. He seldom spoke except to give an order, or to make a terse but memorable comment ('Hard pounding, gentlemen. We will see who can pound the longest') and he took no notice whatever of the shot and shell, except to say once to his conspicuous and gorgeous followers, 'Gentlemen, I think we are a little thick on the ground.' His staff officers were worried about his safety, with good reason, for more than half of them were killed or wounded before the day was out, and if he were hit there was absolutely nobody who could take his place. But none of them dared to suggest he should take

The Duke was on the skyline

more care. Once when he was on horseback right on the skyline watching the French through his telescope, and the shot was whistling round him, one of his aides ventured to take Copenhagen's bridle and lead the patient animal to a safer place; and the Duke seemed not to notice he had moved. In retrospect, it seems unlikely

he was making any effort to preserve the air of calm that people noticed, or to set an example of steadiness to his troops. He did those things, but perhaps quite unconsciously: his mind, it seemed, was so concentrated on the moves in the game he was playing against Napoleon that he really was oblivious of danger, and was thinking of his staff and his army not as men but as pieces, valuable pieces, in the game. In battle, that was his style.

*   *   *

In the matter of style, there could not have been a greater contrast on the other side of the valley. The Emperor was still at Rossomme, still crouched in his old armchair, and still unable—or so it appeared —to concentrate his mind for more than a minute or two at a time on what was happening. It was his habit, more than Wellington's, to leave the conduct of a battle to his high commanders. But at Waterloo he went much further. Until late in the afternoon, he continued to sit there, far out of sight of the most important parts of the battle, a mile and a half from the centre of events. Simply to take a message to him and bring an answer back, through the mud and obstructions on a tiring horse, would have taken a quarter of an hour. Consequently, very little information was sent to him, and in the first six hours of battle he scarcely gave six recorded orders about it, including two of very small importance. Not even he could direct a battle from so far away. It was really Marshal Ney who fought the battle, or the central part of it, and he might have fought it better if the Emperor had not been there at all. For the Emperor was out of touch with events, but Ney was too much in the thick of them, down in the valley, leading the charges, cheering men on and fighting like a trooper. The Emperor could not see into the valley: Ney could not see out of it: from nine in the morning to seven at night they did not see each other. Between them there was a fatally empty post. On the slopes of La Belle Alliance there were positions corresponding to Wellington's, where a commander could have surveyed the whole battle calmly, given his orders quickly and been accessible at once when he was wanted. But there was nobody there.

Ney was under other difficulties too, as crippling in their way as the Emperor's piles. He was a man with all the qualities suggested by his flaming red hair: mercurial, passionate, quick-tempered, brilliant and—as the army itself had called him—the bravest of the brave. People greatly admired his courage, but hardly trusted him: they felt they never knew what he might do next, and they were offended by his manners, which were sometimes brash and boorish. When Paris heard the news of Napoleon's escape from Elba, Ney sallied forth as

Marshal Ney

a royalist general boasting that he would bring Napoleon back to Paris in a cage; but as soon as he met Napoleon's forces he abandoned his own and changed sides. Napoleon found it hard to forgive him for the boastful promise: the royalists never forgave him for failing to carry it out. At first, Napoleon had thought he would be better off without him, but on the eve of leaving Paris to open his campaign, he had sent for him. Ney had only caught up with the army, riding in a borrowed wagon, just before it crossed the frontier. He had only been in command for two days and a half. He did not know his officers, and they did not know exactly what powers the Emperor had given him. So he fought at Waterloo commanded by an ailing, autocratic master who was far away, and commanding a number of generals who were strangers to him and more or less resented his sudden appointment. He did some things which were difficult to explain, but he deserved more sympathy than he was given.

*   *   *

From his forward position, Ney could clearly see the top of Wellington's ridge, but nothing at all beyond it. Presumably he had scouts who looked for points of vantage to watch what was happening on the other side. Sergeant Wheeler, in the sunken lane away beyond the main road to Nivelles, saw a French officer who must either have been a scout or possibly, on the other hand, have wanted to be a deserter. He was all alone, mounted, and at least half a mile away from the rest of his army. Wheeler and two of his men had been put behind a boulder covered with brambles—a safe and comfortable place to watch what was going on. The officer came sneaking along—so it seemed to Wheeler—to look at their position. One of his men was what he called a dead shot within point-blank distance. 'Can you make sure of him?' Wheeler asked. The man said he could. 'But let him come nearer if he will,' he added. 'At all events, his death warrant is signed and in my hands, if he should turn back.' The officer rode close up to them before he saw them. Wheeler's man fired, the officer fell dead, and the three of them dashed out like spiders and dragged his corpse behind their rock. A rich booty, was Wheeler's comment: forty double Napoleons, and they just had time to strip the gold lace off his uniform before they were called away to a new position.

Soon after the disaster of his first attack, the Emperor sent one of his
few specific orders down to Ney: to capture the farm of La Haye
Sainte. And Ney began to assemble two infantry brigades to do it.

La Haye Sainte was an encumbrance in the Duke's position. It
broke the regularity of his line, but it had to be defended because
it was only 200 yards in front of the ridge—close enough to be very
useful to the French if they could take it. He had entrusted its
defence to a detachment of the King's German Legion.

The Legion, the K.G.L. as it was called, was the only body of
foreign troops that the British freely admitted was as good as themselves. The core of it was a force of Hanoverians who had come to
England to carry on the fight when Napoleon had overrun their
own country in 1803. It was a force in the same situation as the Free
French under General de Gaulle, when the Germans overran France
in the Second World War. But its loyalty was less divided, because
the King of England was a Hanoverian himself.

A military exile's life must always be frustrated and melancholy.
For twelve years these men had served in abysmally boring garrisons
and occasional indecisive fights on the borders of Napoleon's empire.
All through the invasion summers of 1804 and 1805, they had
watched on the cliffs and beaches of the south of England for the
fleet that never came. Some had spent a year in Gibraltar, where
nothing happened at all, and some had fought in Denmark, Sweden
and Holland. Most had been in Spain with Wellington, and the
victories there had seemed to bring the end of their exile into sight.
But they had signed on for a period which was to end six months
after the end of the war against Napoleon, and before they were
released and reached their home the escape from Elba had dashed
their hopes again.

Now at Waterloo, confronted at last by Napoleon himself, the
K.G.L. had more to gain and less to lose than most of the men in
Wellington's army. By nightfall, they could expect the course of
their lives to be decided: victory, and an end of those interminable
years, or defeat, and no hope of seeing their homes again.

The brigade which had the responsibility of La Haye Sainte was
stationed on the right of the crossroads, directly behind the farm and
across the main road from Kincaid and the Rifles. It was commanded
by a colonel called Christian von Ompteda, and the detachment in
the farm, 360 men, was under a major named Baring. These two

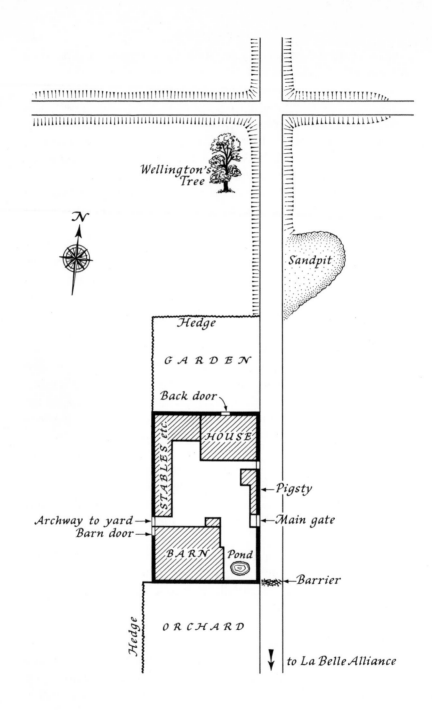

La Haye Sainte

men had been together throughout the twelve years of exile, they knew each other very well, and both were to play conspicuous parts in the battle, Baring first and Ompteda later in the evening. But Baring remains a shadowy figure—the only recorded fact about him is that he had entertained the local gentry in England, years before, by playing the flute. The most complete account of what happened in the farm was given by a young Scottish lieutenant whose name was George Drummond Graeme. Graeme was attached to the German brigade, and he spent most of the afternoon on the roof of a pigsty in the farmyard. There were no pigs in it, but there was a calf which had somehow escaped being killed and eaten the night before.

La Haye Sainte was a smaller, humbler place than Hougoumont, a pretty little farmhouse with its yard enclosed by homely barns and stables. The house was on the north side of the yard, towards the British line, and the garden where Mercer found the potatoes was behind it. A great barn stood on the southern side, and beyond that the orchard. Those two buildings were joined by a range of stables, byres and cartsheds, and the yard was separated from the main road by a high brick wall with a gate in it. There was a pond in the corner of the yard, by the gate, and the pigsty was a lean-to against the inside of the wall. Standing on top of it, looking over the wall, one's head was within a few yards of anyone who came along the road.

Baring, Graeme and their German troops had spent the night there, together with a good many other people sheltering from the rain, but nobody had told them they might have to defend the place. Their pioneers, who carried tools, had been taken away and sent to help at Hougoumont. So they had not made any preparations and, worse still, they had smashed up all the farm carts and chopped the huge barn door to pieces and used them as firewood. There was nothing left to build platforms, the walls were too high to see over, and the barn door gaped wide open across the fields. All they could do in the morning was to drag out branches from the orchard and make a barricade across the road, and to knock a few loopholes in the wall.

Through those, they had a grandstand view of the French infantry columns which had attacked the ridge. One passed them cheering fifty yards away, and of course they blazed away at it with rifles. For a while, the farm was an island surrounded by French cuirassiers

La Haye Sainte in 1816 . . .

and infantry. And then the infantry ran, as Graeme described them, like a flock of sheep. His men were so excited by the British cavalry charge that some of them sallied forth and followed the crowd towards La Belle Alliance. And after it was over, they were surrounded by the dead and dying Frenchmen, the wounded among them still crying out '*Vive l'Empereur!*' in voices that grew more and more feeble. Graeme was distressed to see a man with both legs shattered trying to kill himself with his own sword: he told his servant to take it away from him.

In the lull which followed that attack, when not a single unwounded man was left in the valley, a solitary French cuirassier appeared on the main road near La Belle Alliance and came riding along it waving his sword. Graeme watched him from behind the barricade. Astonished at the sight, he thought he must be a deserter, and he told his own men not to shoot. The horseman rode right up to the barricade, and stood up in his stirrups as if he was looking to

. . . and today

see what was behind it—and then he wheeled his horse and galloped back to the French position. They all fired after him then, but none of them seemed to hit him. Graeme was rather glad to see him get away. What had he intended to do? Perhaps he was suffering—an extreme case—from martial madness, looking for glory in a manner of his own. Perhaps he had gone quite mad. Perhaps he had meant to desert, and had changed his mind. When he reached his regiment again, did he have to explain his pointless escapade, or was he welcomed as a hero? Nobody knows.

It was perhaps a quarter of an hour after that episode when the defenders saw Ney's brigades advancing to attack them. One column was coming up the main road, and one obliquely across the fields. Out on the left, a mass of skirmishers came running among the corpses and threw themselves into the ditch on the other side of the road. Baring withdrew all his men into the building and the yard, abandoning the garden and the orchard. The little farm became a fortress. All round the walls, men fought at point-blank range for every door and window. Across the road, they shot at each other from the loopholes and the ditches. Graeme on top of the pigsty was shooting down the road, to keep them away from the main gate of the yard. But down below him, there was a scuffle at the loopholes, and musket shots came through them from outside: the French had crept along the foot of the wall right under his feet and grabbed the muzzles of the rifles. He could see them behind the barricade he had built himself, and the orchard was swarming with them, right up to the wall of the barn. They rushed at the open doorway, but the Germans inside shot them down until the door was choked with bodies and fresh attackers could not climb over the heap. And the barn caught fire. That seemed the worst threat of all. The barn had been full of straw but most of it had been taken for bedding the night before, and that was luck. A shout went round for water. Baring himself and other officers snatched the camp kettles which some of the men had hanging from their haversacks, rushed into the barn and emptied them on the burning straw, and others followed their lead, ran out again and filled the kettles at the pond. That exposed them to the French, and many fell. But they put out the fire. And the attack began to falter, the musketry died away, they saw the French retreating.

Baring, Graeme, all the defenders, had enough to do to breathe again, to count their dead, bind up their wounded and look to their weapons. They found they had used more than half their ammunition, and Baring sent somebody up to the ridge to ask for more. Yet in the back of their minds, even then, they must have been surprised at the form of the French attack. Why only infantry? Artillery fire from both sides was going over the buildings all the time, and Napoleon's massive battery was only 300 yards away: yet no French gunner had been told to lower his sights for a moment to breach the walls. No doubt La Haye Sainte, like Hougoumont and other Belgian farms, had been built the way it was, facing inwards round its yard, to keep out thieves and wandering marauders. With enough defenders, and enough ammunition, it could keep out infantry too, and stand for ever. But it could not have stood long against artillery and infantry combined.

Perhaps this was a symptom, a small one, of the gap in the French command. Napoleon ordered the place to be taken, and said nothing about the means of doing it. Ney did not ask for a preliminary bombardment. Perhaps he was simply too busy galloping and fighting, perhaps he thought it would only be a waste of time: or perhaps, with more reason, he still believed the Emperor was better informed than he was, and would have specified artillery if he had thought it was needed. Whatever happened, the infantry marched without support to the walls of the farm, and fought there bravely, and died without success.

*   *   *

While that small attack began, flared up and failed, everyone in Wellington's army who could see across the valley was eagerly watching the French and wondering what the next move would be. Telescopes were passed from hand to hand. All the officers were anxious: the Prussians had been expected for the past two hours, but nobody had seen them yet, and the long bombardment was becoming as much as the toughest troops could stand. But what they saw, about four o'clock, surprised them so much that at first they could not believe it. A vast force of cavalry appeared, between the main road and the fields of Hougoumont; and yet there was not a movement to be seen among the enemy's infantry. It looked as if Napoleon was planning an attack by cavalry alone. But nobody had ever heard of an unsupported cavalry attack against an unbroken line of infantry and artillery—and the line, although it was shaken, was far from broken yet. The Duke, who expected brilliant generalship from Napoleon, thought he might be planning a huge outflanking manœuvre to the west beyond Hougoumont, and he sent a brigade of his own cavalry out in that direction. But no: the cuirassiers, followed by lancers and horse chasseurs, were coming to the right of La Haye Sainte and to the left of Hougoumont. It could only be a frontal attack, against the part of the British line between the two farms, the part that had so far seen no fighting and done nothing but suffer inactivity under the gunfire. All along the British line, people discussed it in amazement, and everyone who knew the rules of tactics, from the generals down to the sergeants, formed the same opinion: Bonaparte was trying it too soon, he could not hope to break the line like that, it was suicide for his cavalry. The word went round with almost gleeful confidence—'Prepare to receive cavalry' —and the infantry, lying down behind the ridge, stood up and

Massed Napoleonic cavalry

formed squares in a chequered formation like a chessboard. The Duke said, 'Damn it, the fellow's a mere pounder after all.' And he sent out a peremptory order to the gunners, who were on the forward slope: to maintain their fire as long as possible, and then take refuge inside the squares. Everyone waited.

*   *   *

But the attack had not been ordered by the Emperor. Since the order to take La Haye Sainte, no word of any kind had come down from Rossomme. A grand cavalry attack, supported by the infantry of his Imperial Guard, had been in the Emperor's mind as the culmination of the battle, and he had said so to Ney and his generals in the morning. But it was Ney who was now preparing the attack, and people ever since have wondered why he did it. He must have believed the Duke was on the point of retreating, otherwise it made no sense at all. He had thought so early in the morning and been wrong. Now, through the smoke from the bottom of the valley, the crest of the ridge must have seemed deserted again. And his scouts, if any found a clearer view, may have seen the deserters, the hordes of prisoners and wounded, and the men escorting them, all moving back towards the forest: some of the foremost pickets of the Prussian army saw that sight and mistook it for a general retreat. At all events, Ney sent back an aide to the cavalry generals, to order up a force of cavalry.

But then, through more misunderstandings, the movement seems to have grown into something far bigger than he probably intended. One of the generals sent forward two regiments, but another, more senior, stopped them and sent a message to Ney that he only took his orders from his own corps commander. Ney rode back himself, very angry—and no wonder. He overruled the general, and in his anger—perhaps because of it—he increased his order to include another six regiments of cuirassiers. '*En avance!*' he is said to have shouted. 'The salvation of France is at stake!' And with him at its head, the entire remaining force of Napoleon's cuirassiers began to move forward at a trot.

And then, from a hollow where they had sheltered near La Belle Alliance, the lancers and then the chasseurs of the Imperial Guard, which was not under Ney's command but directly under the Emperor's, came streaming down to the valley behind the cuirassiers. Who ordered them to come? Certainly Ney did not. Perhaps the commander of the cuirassiers asked for their support, or perhaps they joined of their own accord in what promised to be a triumphal exercise. For Ney, when he saw them coming, there was only one possible explanation: that the Emperor had ordered it, that the Emperor knew the British were ready to break and had decided the moment had come for the grand attack. He may well have assumed that the infantry of the Guard, who were out of his sight, were also on the move. And so he found himself, sword in hand, in the proudest position a soldier of France could have filled, leading no less than 12,000 splendid horsemen in fulfilment, as he believed, of

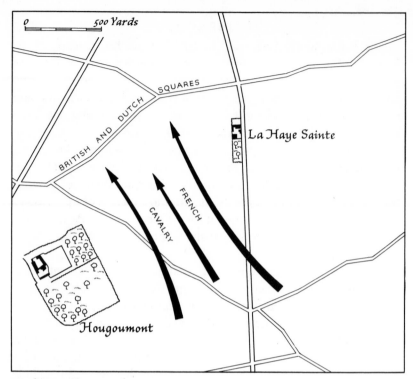

Ney's Cavalry Attack

the Emperor's command, towards the greatest imaginable feat of martial glory.

But the Emperor, sunk in his moody seclusion on the mound at Rossomme, had not given the order and was so far out of touch with events that he had not even seen the movement of his cavalry.

*   *   *

The British who watched were overwhelmed, not by fear but by honest admiration. Everyone who saw the host of horsemen riding up the slope at a slow canter, flowing over the undulations of the ground, was struck by the same simile: the line of them glittered, Gronow wrote, like a stormy wave of the sea when it catches the sunlight. In that line were five hundred abreast, riding stirrup to stirrup, purposeful, deliberate, unhurried and utterly confident in appearance: and behind the front rank were at least a dozen other ranks of equal length. In the gap, a thousand yards wide, between the orchards of La Haye Sainte and Hougoumont, the ranks contracted a little to avoid the musket-fire, and some riders reported afterwards that their horses were lifted off the ground by the pressure. Beyond the farms they expanded again and climbed towards the gunners on the ridge, a spectacle of awful grandeur, Gronow said, which nobody who survived the day could have forgotten in after life. And to the watchers they seemed to come in silence: the roar of the guns drowned every other sound.

Most of the infantry could not see them coming. The first thing they knew was that the French artillery suddenly stopped, and for that they were thankful: nothing else, they thought, could be so bad. But their own artillery just in front of them was still firing down the slope as fast as it could load. And then, battery by battery, that stopped too, and they saw the gunners running back for shelter. And in the silence, their ears still ringing, they heard the pounding of the hoofs and felt it through the ground, and then the shout of triumph as the horsemen overran the guns; and the first of the lines, at the gallop now, came through the gunsmoke over the top of the ridge.

It may have been more of a shock to the French than the British, a shock most of all perhaps to Ney: for the infantry knew that the cavalry was coming, but the cavalry did not know the infantry was there: at fifty paces, instead of a broken line of fugitives, they were confronted by the solid squares of bayonets, the formation it was supposed no cavalry could break. But at those close quarters, the hearts of the British sank. To Gronow, it looked as if nothing could resist the shock of that terrible moving mass. To Sergeant Morris, thoroughly awake, it seemed the British had not the slightest chance. And to Mercer, watching from a distance, still in reserve, the infantry squares seemed to vanish under the flood of horsemen, and he could not believe there would be a man alive when the flood receded.

Afterwards, nobody in the infantry squares had a clear consecutive memory of what happened. They only remembered isolated moments, glimpses through the battle smoke, sudden piercing impressions of sound or smell or sight: the rest was a daze of excitement, fear or horror.

Tom Morris was in the front rank of his regimental square, kneeling with the butt of his musket wedged in the mud beside him, and the muzzles and bayonets of the other two ranks above his head. He clearly remembered the line of horses galloping down on him. They were only a dozen paces away, it seemed to him, when his rear rank fired a volley. Horses came crashing down, their riders fell, some dead, some wounded, some still able to unclasp their heavy armour and run away. The line of them broke, divided and veered aside, and galloped through the spaces each side of the square like a wave of the sea which breaks and eddies round a rock. Morris's rank, and the second rank behind him, fired their volleys, and the sides of the square opened fire too as the horses went charging past them.

Lieutenant Gronow remembered the strange sound of musket-balls against the Frenchmen's breastplates, like a hail-storm beating on windows: the smell of burnt cartridges and the suffocating smoke: the moans of agony of dying men and horses which sickened and appalled him. As a born horseman, he felt for the horses—scarcely less intelligent than the men, he believed, and yet unable to understand the things men thought they were fighting for—now being slaughtered, kicking, struggling or lying mutilated and still in dreadful attitudes, and often raising their heads as if they were looking for their riders, hoping for help.

Yet to shoot at the horses, not at the men, had been the order in Sergeant Lawrence's square, which was next to Gronow's, because the rumour had spread before the battle began that the cavalry's armour was proof against musketry—and indeed it could turn aside a glancing shot. Lawrence was immunized to horror: when the horses fell, it seemed to him a most laughable sight to see the riders trying to run away in what he called their chimney armour. And what he remembered most clearly of the whole awful episode was a macabre joke. His captain, standing beside him, was blown to bits by a shell. A man close by, a notorious character who had always been in trouble with the captain, shouted sarcastically 'Hullo, there goes my best friend.' A lieutenant who stepped forward to take the captain's place heard the shout but missed the point of it. 'Never mind,' he said sententiously, 'I will be as good a friend to you as the captain'—and seemed puzzled by the man's reply, 'I hope not, sir.'

Mercer, watching with his battery in reserve, believed the front line had been totally overwhelmed. He could not see any squares still standing on the ridge, only a few abandoned guns with their muzzles in the air. Everywhere in front of him were horsemen, crossing, turning and riding about in all directions through the smoke without any plan that he could understand. An artillery

colonel who had joined him thought the situation was desperate.
'It does look very bad,' Mercer said, 'but I trust in the Duke, who
I am sure will get us out of it somehow or other.' He would have
said more, but his men could hear him: he was thinking that if the
final catastrophe had come, he would spike his guns and retreat with
all his horses across country, avoiding the main road which he was
certain would be blocked. The horsemen were beginning to come
together in ranks and groups: it seemed the battery itself was about
to be attacked. 'I fear all is over,' the colonel said, and this time
Mercer had to agree. Suddenly, loud shouts to the westward drew
his attention: two dense columns of infantry were marching down
on him. They were not British: he thought they were French, but
he held his fire. An officer rode out to see, came back and said they
were certainly French. Mercer gave the order to fire—and then the
colonel recognized them: they were Belgian. Relieved on that score,
Mercer turned round to look at the ridge again. All the cavalry had
vanished, and none of his men could tell him how or where.

Lord Uxbridge, with the cavalry lines behind the squares, perhaps
had a clearer view than most, and a clearer idea, as a cavalry man, of
what was going to happen. He saw the charging line of the French
break up on the front line of squares, close up again behind it and
break again on the second line. He saw the French regiments mixing,
growing confused and losing their momentum—cuirassiers, lancers
and chasseurs riding round the squares in opposite directions. His own
forces, excepting the Household and Union Brigades, were still in
their battle lines. And he chose his moment for a counter-charge.

Morris was aware of the wave of horsemen receding, the movement turning back towards the ridge, and then he saw the Life
Guards: and men of his regiment forgot themselves for a minute in
watching a hand-to-hand cavalry battle which surged all round them,
a bloody exhibition of horsemanship and swordsmanship. And what
stuck in his mind ever after was a slashing backhand sword-stroke
which sent a cuirassier's helmet flying with his head inside it, and the
horse which galloped away with the headless rider sitting erect in
the saddle.

Lord Uxbridge's cavalry had driven the French back, over the
ridge again and down the slope. The gunners were running out of
the squares, and opening fire wherever the cavalry gave them a
chance. And the moment the ridge was clear of Frenchmen, the

French artillery also opened up: in the squares, the ordeal by cannon
fire began afresh. But not for long. The French re-formed their ranks
and attacked again.

*   *   *

Nobody could even remember afterwards how many times the
cavalry came charging up the slope: officially, it was reckoned there
were twelve attacks. Nor could anyone say how long it lasted:
perhaps it was an hour and a half. In every charge, the same things
happened: the French cavalry overran the guns, but then they lost
formation when they eddied round the squares, and found themselves vulnerable to the musketry and whatever cavalry Lord
Uxbridge could lead against them. Twelve times, the greater part of
the Duke's artillery was in the hands of the French: yet every time,
when the gunners ran out to their guns again, they found them in
working order. Nobody, in the stress of the moment, thought this
was strange. But afterwards, it seemed to most people the strangest
thing in the whole of the battle. In all those twelve attacks, the French
never thought of spiking the British guns. It would have been easy.
All they needed was a handful of headless nails and a hammer: all
they had to do was drive a nail down the touch-hole and the gun was
out of action. It was common practice, and had been so for centuries.
Artillerymen carried nails to do it with, either to spike the enemy's
guns or to spike their own if they had to be abandoned: Mercer had
thought of it as a matter of course. A couple of dozen mounted
artillerymen riding up with the cavalry could have done it in a
minute. Even the cavalry themselves could have broken the wooden
sponge-staves, and that would have made the guns useless before
very long. Or they could have harnessed horses to the guns and
limbers and dragged them away, and Wellington's army would have
been crippled.

But the French did none of these things. Perhaps again the
Emperor was too far away to see the opportunity, and Ney was too
closely involved. For Ney was on the ridge itself, furiously urging
the horsemen on to a task that was impossible—somebody saw him
in a fever of frustration beating on the muzzle of a British gun with
the flat of his sword. But the Emperor was only watching through
his telescope. At first, he was reluctant to believe the horsemen he
could see on the ridge were his own. Some of his staff, convinced

'*Here comes the Calvary*'

that they were, thought victory was won. But he was wiser. 'This is a premature movement,' he said to his chief of staff, 'and it may have fatal results in the course of the day.' Marshal Soult agreed, and put the blame on Ney. 'It is an hour too soon, but we must stand by what is already done,' the Emperor added. And he ordered forward another four brigades of cavalry—a useless addition: already there were so many horsemen on the narrow front that none of them were able to manœuvre.

* * *

Every time the French came thundering up the slope, the man next to Morris said 'Tom, Tom, here comes the calvary'—and every time he got the word wrong. Morris believed the French were turning the British guns round and firing at his square at point-blank range, and he even had a mental picture afterwards of French artillerymen with the slow matches in their hands. Nobody else reported that, and probably he was mistaken. But shells and grape-shot certainly came from somewhere, blasting lanes right through the square. The men on both sides of him fell, the man who said 'calvary' got a ball through his thigh and died of it later, and Morris had a piece of cast iron which lodged in his cheek so that the blood ran down inside his clothes. The old captain, thirty-two years in the army and never in action before, was horribly frightened—so Morris

Horse artillery on the move

said—and came to him several times for a drop of something to keep his spirits up: but he was blown to bits before the day was out. Yet every time the grape-shot blasted gaps in the square, the infantry closed them, dragging the wounded into the square and throwing the dead outside, before the cavalry could ride through them.

French lancers were killing what British and German wounded they happened to see. A mounted swordsman could not easily reach a wounded man who was lying on the ground, but a lancer could do it with horrifying ease, a mere gesture of the heavy lance as he rode by. It angered the British who saw it almost beyond control—such a blatant disregard for what they thought were the decencies of war. It angered them just as much when their allies did it. Gronow saw a colonel of the French Hussars fall under his horse, and while he struggled to free himself two Brunswick soldiers ran out of the neighbouring square and took his purse, his watch and his pistols —and then they put the pistols to his head and blew his brains out. A shout of 'Shame!' went up from the British square. But the British, so illogically merciful to men who were wounded, were

utterly merciless to anyone who was not, whatever his situation.
Sergeant Wheeler, still in the sunken lane beyond the Nivelles road,
saw nearly a hundred horsemen coming along it at full gallop: they
must have passed through the squares, and rather than ride back
through the musketry fire were looking for a way round the end
of the British line. But the lane had been blocked by branches.
Unable to climb the banks, and unable to turn because of the others
pressing on behind, they came to a halt jammed together as tightly
as so many horses could be. Wheeler and his companions, manning
the road block, fired a single volley. By the time they had loaded
again and the smoke had cleared, one man, and only one, was
running away. One other was taken prisoner. For curiosity, Wheeler
went to see what had happened to the rest. The men who were shot
dead were lucky, he thought, for the wounded horses, plunging and
kicking, were finishing what the musketry had begun. He could not
see a single man he thought was likely to recover, and as he had other
business to attend to, he left them to their fate.

It must have been after the first charge that Mercer was ordered

French cavalry faced by a British square

up to the front line on the ridge. Sir Augustus Fraser, who commanded the horse artillery, came galloping up with his face as black as a chimney sweep's and his sleeve torn open by a musket shot. 'Left limber up, and as fast as you can!' he shouted. Mercer gave the order, 'At a gallop, march!' and away they went. (The Duke himself saw them from a distance: 'Ah! that's the way I like to see horse artillery move,' he said.) Fraser rode up with Mercer, and repeated the Duke's order: in a cavalry charge, do not expose your men but retire into the squares. Coming fresh to the ridge, Mercer noticed the air was suffocatingly hot like an oven, and above the roar of cannon and musketry he heard a humming noise, like myriads of black beetles on a summer night. He knew what it was, the cannon shot, the grape and musket-balls. But his battery surgeon had never heard the infernal music before, and Mercer laughed at his astonishment. 'My God, Mercer, what *is* that? What *is* all this noise? How curious! How very curious!' And then, when a cannon shot rushed hissing past, 'There! There! What is it all?'

The troop galloped into position between two squares of young Brunswick soldiers—only boys, Mercer thought. They were standing like logs while the shot made great gaps in their squares, and their officers and sergeants were physically pushing them together to close the gaps and thumping them to make them move. They seemed to be at breaking point; if they see us run, he thought, they will run too. And he made up his mind to stick to his guns whatever happened, and neglect the order the Duke had given.

There was no more time to think: the cavalry were not a hundred yards away, coming out of the smoke at a brisk trot, Grenadiers in blue: their broad brown belts and huge muff caps made them seem gigantic. 'Form line for action! Case-shot!' he shouted, and the guns drew up behind a little bank, the muzzles hardly above the level of the ground. The first round brought down men and horses, the Brunswickers opened musket fire, and the other guns came into action one by one. Even to Mercer, the effect seemed terrible—the ground instantly covered by a struggling mass of wounded. It slowed the whole body of them to a walk, but still they came slowly on, the second and third ranks picking their way through the bodies, his men reloading, ramming and firing again. Now at a few yards, every shot of the case hit something: the leaders hesitated, turned aside and rode away to the flanks, exposing the ranks which were following. But the mass of horsemen could not suddenly retreat. Some turned about and tried to ride back through the body of the column: the guns fired again and again, the men who had ridden up so superbly became a mob, struggling with each other, using the pommels of their swords to fight a way through their own comrades, still falling in scores at every blast of shot. Some, desperate at finding themselves pent up before the guns, charged through them, and some were carried past by bolting horses maddened by their wounds. For a minute or two of appalling slaughter, the column was held there, imprisoned by its own size and weight: and then the rear ranks wheeled about and opened a passage, and the whole mass of it swept away down the slope and into cover. Mercer's men ceased fire, but reloaded and stood ready: beyond the ridge, they could still see the tops of the high caps of the enemy. This time, they double-loaded, with ball and case-shot on top of it, the shortest-range and most lethal of the artillery's devices.

There was a warning of the next charge. A swarm of skirmishers ran up the hill, taking cover behind the corpses, and started a galling fire with muskets and pistols at scarcely forty paces. The artillery had no reply to that: they had no small arms, and had to stand still with their slow matches lighted and be shot at. Mercer saw them growing restive, and feared they would be goaded into letting fly and wasting ammunition; and it was then that he put his horse at the bank in front of the battery and rode up and down to quieten his men and draw the skirmishers' fire on himself, calling them by all the insulting names in French he could remember, and trusting to luck that even at forty paces none of them would hit him. And none of them did.

The squadrons came again, at the same steady trot, more numerous, it seemed, than ever: not a furious galloping charge, but a deliberate advance, at the measured pace of men determined to carry their way. Before, they had shouted and cheered: now they came in grim silence. And the gunners waited, also grim and silent. This time, a French officer rode ahead in a rich uniform, covered with decorations on the breast, and he alone was shouting and waving his sword: perhaps it was Ney. Mercer had a moment to reflect that only his own word was wanted to hurl destruction on that splendid show of gallant men and horses. He had confidence now. He let them come until the head of the column was fifty yards away—the rear of it still out of sight below the brow. Then he shouted 'Fire!'

'The squadrons came again'

The effect was instant and dreadful. Nearly the whole leading rank was scythed down by the case-shot, and the round-shot penetrated the column and carried confusion through the depths of it. The ground, already encumbered with the victims of the earlier charge, became almost impassable. But still, the riders struggled over the rampart of dead and wounded, intent on reaching the guns. It was impossible. Some cleared everything and rode through the battery, some came plunging forward to fall at the muzzles of the guns; but the mass of them tried in vain to urge their horses over the gruesome obstacle. The officer, still shouting them on, was unhurt. But with the same confusion, the same struggle among themselves, the survivors retreated over the brow of the hill. And with their retreat, as ever, the French artillery began again.

'Damn it, Mercer,' a voice said, 'you have hot work of it here': Sir George Adam Wood, the veteran commander of artillery, appeared through the smoke and shellfire. He was blinking, Mercer observed, as a man does when he is facing a gale of wind. 'Yes, sir, pretty hot,' Mercer said with soldierly modesty, and began to give the general an account of what had happened. But he had to interrupt it—'There they are again!' the leading squadrons once more were on the ridge, riding forward again at the same fatal spot. Mercer could admire their bravery and persistence, and almost feel sorry for them. It was folly to attempt the thing, he thought. For his gunners, it was child's play now to shoot them down, they could not possibly approach in good order across the wall of their own dead. Seeing them turn defeated to retire again, he was intoxicated by his own success and was crying out 'Beautiful, beautiful!' and flourishing his sword. Someone behind him seized his sword arm and said, 'Take care, or you'll strike the Duke'—and the Duke himself rode past in front of the battery, which abruptly had to cease fire. He looked tired and serious, and seemed not to take the slightest notice of the remnants of the enemy cavalry still charging about to find a way of escape.

*   *   *

The Duke had been in the thick of it all the time, riding along the line and taking shelter inside the squares each time the cavalry charged. Most of the infantry must have seen him, outwardly composed and calm, apparently unconscious of the carnage which surrounded him. Some people heard his terse remarks, or thought they did. Gronow saw him sitting unmoved on his charger, thoughtful and pale, and heard him ask a colonel what o'clock it was. The colonel took out his watch and said it was twenty minutes past four, and the Duke replied, 'The battle is mine, and if the Prussians arrive soon, there will be an end of the war.' But Gronow must have misheard him: nobody, least of all the Duke, could have been so brashly confident. Morris heard a more probable exchange when the Duke rode into his square. 'Well, Halket,' he said to the general, 'how do you get on?' 'My Lord, we are dreadfully cut up. Can you not relieve us for a little while?' 'Impossible,' said the Duke. 'Very well, my Lord,' said the general, 'we'll stand till the last man falls.' And that was not a figure of speech. It seemed to be only a matter of time.

*   *   *

After Lord Uxbridge's first successful counter-charge, the infantry expected the same success to be repeated every time, but it was not. They began to grumble, as one arm of an army often does, and ask what the other arm was doing. And they had some reason: things had gone wrong in the allied cavalry.

Lord Uxbridge had had an ignominious experience. The British heavy cavalry was terribly thinned and exhausted by its earlier charges, and a light cavalry charge which he led had not had much success. But there were still large numbers of foreign cavalry who had not been in action yet. Uxbridge knew very little about them, not even the names of their officers. They had been under the Prince of Orange, but the Prince had asked the Duke that very morning, just before the battle began, to put them all under Uxbridge's command. Now, in the desperate moment of the French attacks, he saw a column of Dutch cavalry, magnificently accoutred and splendid in appearance. He galloped back to them, called on them to charge, and led the charge in person. Luckily, an aide-de-camp at full gallop caught him up before he reached the enemy and told him there was nobody behind him. The Dutchmen were standing stolidly in their ranks. Uxbridge was naturally angry, and the British in general blamed the Dutch for cowardice. But possibly none of them, except their most senior officers, knew who Lord Uxbridge was. They may not have seen any obvious reason to follow an excited Englishman who gave his orders in a language they could hardly understand and galloped madly at a force of several thousand French.

There was less excuse by any military standard for a regiment of Cumberland Hussars, who were Hanoverians. During the French attacks, Lord Uxbridge saw that regiment leaving the field and quietly riding away towards the forest. He sent an aide-de-camp to tell it to halt. The aide-de-camp found the colonel of the regiment and delivered the order, and the colonel gave the unusual reply that he had no confidence in his own men, they were volunteers, and their horses were their own property. The regiment marched on. The aide-de-camp, who was a captain, told the colonel what he thought of him, and even seized the bridle of his horse and tried to turn it—insults worth a court martial or a duel. But nothing would stop them. The whole regiment rode away to Brussels, right through the city and beyond, shouting to everyone they saw that the battle was lost and the French were coming: and no doubt they believed it was true.

*   *   *

Slowly, around the squares of infantry, a kind of stalemate came about, a state of affairs that nobody had seen before in battle. The cavalry was irresistible, but the squares were immovable. Even the Duke was astonished. 'We had the French cavalry walking about us as if they had been our own,' he said afterwards. 'I never saw the British infantry behave so well.' The infantry in fact had learned by repeated experience to welcome the cavalry, because when they were there the artillery stopped, and the cavalry was much the less dangerous of the two. And they also learned that when they fired a volley, the cavalry tried to break through them before they could reload. So they stopped firing. On the other hand, the ground had been so cut up, and so encumbered with corpses, that the cavalry could not charge, or move at more than a trot. For the most part, they only walked, prowling round the squares and looking for any chance to break in. Often they halted, and French and British stood staring at each other, and neither side could think of anything fresh to do. Men in the squares came to know the faces of the French after seeing them so many times. The huge attack, with the thousands of men on each side, broke down into scattered individual contests, each watched by hundreds of men who had nothing to do. A cuirassier walked his horse right up to the point of Morris's bayonet, leaned out of the saddle and made a cut at him with his sword. Morris could not avoid it, and shut his eyes. When he opened them, the man was lying in front of him on the ground: a rear-rank man had wounded and unhorsed him. There at Morris's feet he tried to kill himself with his own sword. It was too long. He dropped it and took a bayonet that was lying there, raised himself with one hand, put the point of the bayonet under his cuirass and fell on it.

That classic gesture of despair might stand as a symbol of Napoleon's cavalry, when at last its survivors rode down the slope and were ordered to abandon the attack. They had met their match. Thrown into the battle without the support of infantry, they had fought to the death with blind unquestioning bravery and achieved absolutely nothing, except to add vastly to the sum of suffering. For the Emperor, the attack had wasted time that he could not afford, and had crippled the cavalry for ever: its failure had opened the cracks in his army's resolution. For the British and their allies, the losses of life and limb had been as bad or worse: the insides of the squares were like hospitals or morgues. But they had gained the time that the French had lost and—which was more—they had proved their own courage to themselves. They had won the round, and were proud of it. Desperately few of them were left. But probably, after they saw the cavalry ride away, nothing short of annihilation could have shifted the remnants off the ridge.

EVENING

Surgeons—Fall of La Haye Sainte
Crisis in the centre
The Prussians arrive
The attack of the Garde Impérial
Victory and defeat

EVENING

In cottages and barns on both sides of the battlefield, surgeons were busy with their knives and saws. Most of the wounded still lay where they had fallen, but enough had walked or been carried off the field to overwhelm the medical services.

It is easy now to look on the surgery of 1815 as mere butchery. But each generation is satisfied with the medical treatment of its own time, and men will always die for lack of discoveries made soon after they are dead. At Waterloo, there were no antiseptics and no anaesthetics: both were in the future. But it was a time when army surgery was improving quickly. People could still remember the days when no treatment at all was given to the wounded, who were largely left to the care of the local population, whether it was friendly or not. Not very long before, the great surgeon John Hunter had written that 'it was hardly necessary for a man to be a surgeon to practise in the army.' And John Hennen, who was a surgeon at Waterloo, remembered that in his own early days army surgery was looked on as 'the lowest step of professional drudgery and degradation. If a man of superior merit by chance sprung up in it, he soon abandoned the employment for the more lucrative, the more respectable, and the less servile work of private practice.' By 1815, there were still some very bad surgeons in the army, but there were some good ones too, who were working on the frontiers of the knowledge of their day. So a soldier looking back on his father's time could think himself lucky.

Napoleon's doctor, Baron Larrey, was recognized even by the British as the foremost of army surgeons. He had invented what he called the flying ambulance, which was a light, well-sprung two-wheeled cart fitted with litters: it was intended to take the wounded off the field and bring them quickly to the hospitals. In the French army, each division had twelve of these ambulances, with four heavy wagons for medical supplies and 130 medical staff, all of whom were mounted. During the lull while Napoleon was in Elba, there had been some contact between the professions in Britain and France, but the British had not had time to introduce these new ideas. They had no special transport for wounded, and the surgeons, except the most senior, had no trained assistants. In battle, the musicians of regimental bands were often the first to be told to carry the wounded to the surgeons, and hold them during operations, and lay them in improvised hospitals afterwards.

A British surgeon carried his own outfit of knives, scalpels, saws, spare blades for the saws, tourniquets, forceps and strops to sharpen the knives on. These were fitted in a wooden case lined with plush, and kept bright with linseed oil. Beyond this, a recommended list of necessities was the following: lint, surgeon's tow, sponges, linen, both loose and in rollers, silk and wax for ligatures, whalebone splints, pins, tape, thread, needles, adhesive plaster ready coated, opium, both solid and in tincture, submuriate of mercury, antimonials, sulphate of magnesia, volatile alkali, oil of turpentine, wax candles, phosphoric matches, and a canteen of good wine or spirits diluted; for as a medical handbook said, 'Many men sink beyond recovery for want of a timely cordial before, during and after operations.'

Soldiers at least knew what to expect if they were wounded and reached the surgeons alive: there was nothing esoteric or complex in

Baron Larrey's flying ambulance

their treatment. For chest or abdominal wounds, nothing could be done except plaster or stitch the external wound together and wait to see what happened. Extensive abdominal operations had been performed by civil surgeons, but the chance of survival was so small that no surgeon in battle would think of wasting time on them. For legs or arms, however, there was a ready remedy: cut them off. Soldiers believed that surgeons lopped off arms and legs by the cart-load to save themselves trouble. There was some truth in that. It did save trouble, both for the surgeons and the patients. The round missiles were so destructive that amputation was best for anything more than a simple fracture or a flesh wound that had missed the main arteries. Some surgeons claimed nine successes out of ten for amputations promptly carried out, if they were below the middle of the thigh: above that, they were dangerous, though men with legs removed at the hip-joint had sometimes survived. It was laid down as a principle of military surgery that no lacerated joint, particularly knee, ankle or elbow, should leave the field unampu-tated, unless the patient was obviously going to die. And soldiers themselves approved this practice: most of them, brought in with smashed arms or legs, wanted them off at once.

In that respect, the soldiers were in advance of medical opinion. For years, there had been arguments in the profession about the best time to amputate—immediately after the injury, or two or three days later, when the patient had recovered from the shock, or weeks later when the local inflammation had subsided—if it did. The

surgeons of Wellington's army **in** Spain had slowly come to agree
with the soldiers' view, that it was best to get it over quickly. By the
time of Waterloo, they preferred to 'lop off' the limbs as soon as the
patients were brought to them, unless they were in a serious state of
shock: then warmth and a glass of wine were used to prepare them.
But however fast they worked that afternoon there were always
hundreds waiting for their turn.

   Apart from the amputations, most of the surgeon's work was in
probing for foreign bodies, setting simple fractures and bandaging.
Probing was done with the bare fingers, and special forceps were
made to fit musket-balls. Extraction was thought to be simpler if the
patient was in the same position he had been in when he was hit.

Usually, therefore, he was made to stand up if he could; but some surgeons went to the length of putting their cavalry patients on the back of a horse before they began to probe. The round musket-balls took unexpected courses. One man at Waterloo was hit on his adam's apple: the ball went harmlessly right round his neck inside the skin, and came back to where it had started. Odd things were sometimes extracted: cloth, leather, coins which the patients said were not their own, and bits of other people's bones and teeth. It always encouraged a patient, one surgeon noticed, when the bullet could be extracted and given to him as a souvenir.

The only positively mistaken practice at Waterloo was bleeding. No precautions were taken against sepsis, because nobody knew what caused it, but the archaic remedy of bleeding was still in use for preventing or curing fevers, and even men who had lost a lot of blood from their wounds were repeatedly bled by the surgeons. The appearance of the blood was important in prognosis. Soldiers believed they were more fit to recover from wounds because the meagre army diet kept their blood thin. A crowd of city aldermen in a battle, they said, would die of their wounds because their blood would be too rich.

The most surprising thing to the modern mind is that men would submit to the probing, stitching, cutting and sawing, without any kind of anaesthetic, yet without any overwhelming dread. The wine and diluted spirits the surgeons carried were given, in moderate doses, to strengthen the patients, not to make them insensible: the opiates were to rest them after the operation, not before. One surgeon, discussing broken bones, wrote that 'after the action of Waterloo, the excruciating torture brought on by the slightest attempt at setting the limbs was in some instances very remarkable'. It would seem less remarkable now, for he was in Brussels, and his patients had had their broken legs and arms set twice before, once on the field and again at Mont St. Jean, and then had been carried in unsprung carts across a dozen miles of cobbled roads. Men in those days, one must suppose, were not less sensitive to pain than they are now. But pain was familiar, in themselves and others. So they were less afraid of it than later generations, brought up with anaesthetics; and perhaps the fear of pain is exaggerated now, in people who have never had a serious pain and know it can be avoided. Besides that, it was part of a soldier's code to go through an amputation with an

air of unconcern. A French prisoner who picked up his sawn-off leg
and threw it into the air shouting '*Vive l'Empereur*' was thought
eccentric by the British who happened to see him. But everyone
admired an officer at Mont St. Jean who refused to be helped from
the table when his leg had been cut off, but jumped down and
hopped unaided to the cart that was waiting to take him to Brussels.
And there was always a final compensation: a wooden leg was a
lifelong badge of courage.

*   *   *

Five o'clock: down in the outpost of La Haye Sainte, Major Baring
and his Germans were counting their ammunition. They had been
firing all day, not only at the troops who attacked them in the farm,
but also at the columns of cavalry and infantry which passed them to
attack the main position. Baring had sent four messengers up to the
ridge to ask for ammunition, but none had come: instead, he was sent
reinforcements of men. About six o'clock, he sent a final urgent
request: unless supplies came soon, the farm would fall.

Nobody else in Wellington's army had run short of ammunition,
although they used prodigious quantities—Mercer, who was not in
action all the time, fired 700 nine-pounder rounds per gun. Even
Hougoumont was well supplied. When the garrison there began to
run short they told a staff officer who had come down with a message,
and on his way back to the ridge he saw an ammunition wagon with
one corporal in charge of it. He told the corporal, and the corporal
set off without any orders full speed across the fields, right through
the hottest fire, and reached Hougoumont alive with the wagon.

But La Haye Sainte, the key to the centre of Wellington's line,
was left without supplies all day. Nobody ever discovered what had
gone wrong: almost everyone who might have known was dead
before the day was out. Afterwards, somebody told the Duke there
was no way into the farm except by the gate from the road or
another one on the opposite side from the fields, and that both those
entrances were under fire from the French. The people who made
that excuse said Baring ought to have knocked a hole in the wall of
the house on the side which faced the British lines; and the Duke said
he ought to have seen to it himself, but had not been able to think of
everything. But the excuse was quite untrue. There was a door from

the house into the garden, and it was seldom under fire. If the only difficulty was to get there, somebody had been faint-hearted. A more plausible explanation, perhaps, was that the Germans had rifles, not muskets, so that they needed a special ammunition, and that all their reserves of it were in a single wagon which was overturned and stuck in the chaos on the Brussels road.

The Germans were intrepid soldiers. Already, in the farm, there were far more dead than living, but they had held the place all day and were sure they could hold it till night, if only somebody would send a few knapsacks of bullets and cartridges down from the ridge. By six, when the cavalry attacks came finally to an end, they had searched the pockets and pouches of their dead and wounded and shared all they could find among the living—and it came to four rounds per man. It was grossly unfair. Soldiers who have fought with all their skill, and risked their lives and seen their friends lose theirs, suffer a special frustration when they are not given what they need to fight with: a man who has made up his mind to die for a cause is all the more unwilling to die through inefficiency. So these survivors suffered. They cursed and complained to Baring and Graeme, and Baring and Graeme would have done the same if there had been anyone there they could complain to. But the men still said they were willing to fight it out, and not one of them deserted.

In the stillness after the cavalry attacks, they heard and saw what every one of them knew was their doom approaching: fresh columns of infantry marching up on them, as they had before, across the fields and along the road. Ney, abandoning the cavalry assault, had reverted to the order the Emperor had given him three hours before: to take the farm at all costs. Before, he had failed: this time he could not fail. As the French soldiers warily advanced towards the orchard, the farm remained silent. The silence must have told them something was wrong: their experience probably told them what it was. Once more they swarmed up to the walls, against the few last scattered shots the defenders could muster. Some entered the barn, where so many had fallen before, and set it on fire again. Some broke in by a door to the yard, but they were killed with bayonets as they came. Some rushed the main gate with an axe. Graeme's men on top of the pigsty shot them down with their last remaining rounds, but whenever the man with the axe was hit, another picked it up. Then Graeme heard shots from behind: the French had climbed up to the

In the yard of La Haye Sainte

roof of the stables opposite and were firing into the yard at point-blank range, and the men in the yard had nothing left to shoot with. It was hopeless. Baring gave the order to retire. There was only one way left—through the house and out of the door to the garden.

The axe smashed down the gate, and the French poured into the yard. Graeme jumped down from his roof and ran for his life across to the front door of the house. There was a narrow hallway inside, and a dozen men in it. He thought of rallying there and making a charge, but shots came down the passage behind him. A young ensign called Frank who was there before him shouted a warning, and he saw a man aiming a musket at him: Frank rushed at the man and stabbed him before he fired. But more came running in. A French officer grabbed Graeme by the collar and shouted '*C'est ce coquin*', and four men levelled their bayonets at him. He parried them with his sword, and shook off the officer's grip. Frank had gone, and so had everyone else. And then he saw that the Frenchmen looked frightened, and as pale as ashes. 'You shan't keep me,' he thought, and he bolted for the back door. Two shots came after him, but nobody followed him.

Ensign Frank was shot in the arm and he had run too, but to the wrong door. He was in a bedroom, with no way out of it. He hid under the bed, and stayed there all the rest of the day. Two wounded soldiers were also in the room: the French found them, and shot them there. Graeme escaped to the ridge, though he was also wounded. So did Baring. And so did thirty-nine more of the 360 who had garrisoned the farm that morning. But that was all.

*   *   *

The loss of the farm brought the whole of Wellington's army very near disaster. As the lucky survivors came running or limping up the hill, the French came close behind, and the brunt of the attack fell suddenly, at the closest range, on the German brigade from which they had been detached. Its commander, Christian von Ompteda, just on the right of the crossroads, saw the French infantry massed in the hedge of the farmhouse garden 200 yards in front of him. He saw French artillery under cover of the buildings, brought up within grape-shot range. The helmets of a force of cuirassiers were showing, in a dip to the right of the farm. And then a cloud of skirmishers pressed even closer, under a little mound above the garden, eighty yards from the centre of Wellington's line, and opened a blaze of musketry. Ompteda's own men were sheltered by the sunken lane, but they had suffered so much already that wide gaps in his part of the line were undefended. The British brigade on his right was in no better shape, and there were no reserves behind him. On his left, across the main road, Kincaid and the Rifle Brigade were face to face with the enemy hidden behind the mound, and they had no protection except the hedges of the lane which already were trampled down and shot to pieces. And at that moment, a mistake in tactics was to make the line still thinner.

For Wellington, the army, and the cause they were fighting for, it was a moment of desperate crisis: for Christian von Ompteda himself, it was the climax of a lifetime of soldiering and twelve years of hope frustrated and deferred. He had been one of the first of the Hanoverians who volunteered to go to England in order to fight against Napoleon. He had suffered all the boredom, disappointment, and loneliness of exile. He had spent years on the south coast of England, longing for a chance to do something to set his own country free, quartered in tents and damp turf huts which destroyed his health, drilling his men to a point of meticulous perfection. In those years, he had learned to know the English well. He liked them and got on well with them. But to live in a free country where even the humblest people had an undefeated national pride and a sense of belonging—this had constantly wounded him and reminded him of his own country's defeat and the petty tyranny of the French who ruled it. The melancholy life had driven him twice into nervous breakdowns; but each time, when he recovered, he took up the same life again.

There was a curious personal reason too, beyond mere patriotism, in Ompteda's longing to see his country free. He was a kindly, gentle, introspective man by nature. He had never married. Before he left home, he had twice fallen in love with married women, who loved him in return but would not or could not leave their husbands. In exile, he did not look for another woman to love, but he gave to his two brothers all the affection and care which he might, in a happier life, have given a wife and children. Both of them were married, and consequently had to stay behind in Hanover. All through those twelve years, he had written them letters: letters which had to be sent by devious secret routes and expressed in guarded terms in case they were intercepted by the French—letters full of outspoken German sentiment which Englishmen of his time would have found embarrassing. He had longed above everything else to see his two brothers again. But now, at Waterloo, he had recently heard that one of them was dead. It had reminded him that all of them were ageing, that time was running out for them. He had written at once that he would like to look after the dead man's two sons, and when he came to Belgium they had contrived to come out of Hanover, through Holland, and join him there. They were with him on the battlefield, two symbols of the family unity he was fighting to regain. The younger was only fifteen.

This, then, was Colonel von Ompteda's private cause in the battle: he could expect to know, by the time the sun went down, whether he could hope to live at home again, or only look forward to a lonely old age in exile. And suddenly, the weight of the French attack was on his own brigade, the outcome of the battle seemed largely to be on his shoulders. He knew precisely what he had to do. That part of the line was his to defend, and he had to defend it while any of his men were still alive. Twenty years of military life had made him ready for the task.

It was that moment that the twenty-two-year-old general, the Prince of Orange, chose to give an order. One of his aides came galloping up to Ompteda and told him to deploy a battalion in line and advance against the skirmishers. This was such madness that Ompteda queried it. He pointed out the French cavalry under cover two or three hundred yards away, waiting for just such an opportunity. His men were in a good defensive position they might hope to hold. If they left it to advance in line, they could not be half way to the farm before they were destroyed. The aide rode away, but soon the Prince himself came riding up, bringing Ompteda's corps commander, General von Alten. Alten repeated the order, and Ompteda pointed again to the French cavalry, suggested advancing in square instead of line, and asked if there were any cavalry support. On that, the young Prince insisted that the cavalry all of them could see were Dutch—and it dawned on the officers assembled that he had given the otherwise senseless order in the belief that the horsemen down by the farm were his own. It was inconceivable that any Dutch cavalry could have been standing passively there in formation, well behind the French front line. But it was a forgivable mistake in a young man who had never seen the heat and confusion of a battle. They persuaded him he was wrong. But to be caught in a foolish mistake had stung the Prince's pride. Everyone, shocked into silence, heard him say in a sharp and peremptory voice: 'I must still repeat my order to attack in line with the bayonet, and I will listen to no further arguments.'

By every rule of the military code, there was only one thing that Ompteda could do: he could only carry out the order—and having sent his men to a useless death, he could not in honour come back alive himself. He said to one of his lieutenant-colonels 'Take care of my nephews if you can,' and then he drew his sword, gave the order to deploy, and rode out in front of the line.

Kincaid was watching from across the road, and he saw what happened. The German infantry climbed out of the sunken lane and marched down the slope in line abreast. The skirmishers fell back

The Prince of Orange

before them and vanished into the hedges of the garden of the farm. And the cuirassiers came charging round the corner of the garden, took the line of men end-on and rode it down. Kincaid's men had their rifles levelled but they could not fire for fear of hitting the Germans. Some British light dragoons, seeing the incredible manœuvre, charged down the slope to try to save the Germans, but it was all too quick. It seemed to Kincaid that every man in the line was put to death in about five seconds. Then the rifles fired and drove away both forces of cavalry, and the field where hundreds of men had been fighting was suddenly still again.

Ompteda's lieutenant-colonel had grabbed the two boys who were following their uncle and pushed them back protesting into the lane. Ompteda himself had been seen riding down alone towards the farm ahead of everybody. Scores of muskets were aimed at him from the garden hedge, but the French seemed to be astonished at the solitary approach of a senior officer, and seemed to hold their fire. He put his horse at the hedge and jumped into the garden. People saw his sword flashing before he sank from his horse and vanished. His body was found that evening. A singed hole in his collar showed he had been shot at point-blank range.

*   *   *

The loss of that whole battalion left another gap. At that moment, the centre of the line could not possibly have stood against a French advance. A staff officer named Kennedy galloped off to warn the Duke and found him at the right-hand end of the line, beyond the Nivelles road. Over there, the line was also under fire from skirmishers, and so was he: he had just given one of his most laconic orders—'Drive those fellows away!' He received the news with his usual calm. 'I shall order the Brunswick troops to the spot,' he told Kennedy. 'Go you and get all the German troops to the spot that you can, and all the guns that you can find.' Kennedy did his best. Behind Kincaid, some infantry were brought up and formed into square to cover the main road, in case the French broke through and marched along it. Behind them, the remains of the Union and Household Brigades of cavalry were formed in a single line, to make them look stronger than they were. 'Where is your brigade?' someone asked Lord Edward Somerset. 'Here,' he said, and pointed to a few score of horsemen, and to the ground covered with dying men and mutilated horses wandering and turning round in circles—all that remained of the 2,000 sabres who had charged the French that morning.

Over the scene of death and despair the gunsmoke hung and thickened. Eighty yards away, Kincaid could soon only see the French by the flash of their muskets. Some people noticed a lull of a minute or two when hardly a shot was fired, because neither side could see the enemy. Kincaid began to wonder if a battle had ever ended with everyone killed on both sides. He was on foot by then, his horse had so many wounds he had had to dismount and let it go, and he walked along the ridge in the hope of getting a glimpse of what was going on. But he could see nothing, except the bodies and wreckage.

The Duke himself rode into the breach at the head of the Brunswickers. Many officers sought him out to make the same report: their forces were so cut up that they could not hold their positions. He offered them nothing, no reinforcements and no retreat, no alternative but to stand where they were till they died. But even divisional generals were talking of retreat. None of them meant to retreat, but they had to agree what to do if somebody else retreated and the whole line suddenly broke to pieces. That seemed imminent. Everyone waited for the skirmishers' fire to die away, and for the drum-beats of the *pas de charge* which would herald a new French column marching through the smoke—a column they knew they would not be able to resist. 'Night or the Prussians must come,' the Duke was heard to say.

*   *   *

It may have been then, or may have been rather earlier, that Sir William De Lancey was hit. He was riding with the Duke, as he had been all day, and a cannon ball bounded up off the ground and struck him in the back. The blow threw him many yards over the head of his horse. He fell on his face, jumped up and fell again. All the staff dismounted and ran to him. The Duke, who had known him since he was a boy, went and took his hand. 'Pray tell them to leave me and let me die in peace,' he said. A cousin of his named De Lancey Barclay had seen him fall, and tried to persuade him to be taken to

the rear, in case he was crushed by artillery or captured by the enemy. He asked to be left on the ground and said it was impossible he could live, but Barclay insisted, and called some soldiers to carry him in a blanket. They took him to the surgeons' post in the farm of Mont St. Jean. He asked Barclay to come close to him, and begged him to write to his wife Magdalene at Antwerp, to say everything kind and break the news as gently as he could: and he gave him some personal messages for her. Barclay believed the farm might soon be captured, so he told the soldiers to carry Sir William farther back to the village. They did so, and left him alone in a cottage, and went back to their posts. So nobody knew where he was, and the Duke and his friends had given him up for dead.

*   *   *

Now, at the time when the help of the Prussians was needed most urgently, they were marching not towards the ridge, but away.

The Duke knew that Blücher was attacking Napoleon's flank down in the village of Plancenoit. But this was not even in sight from the middle of the ridge—the spire of the village church could be seen from the left-hand end of the line, but that was all. He did not know how heavy the attack was, or how successful. At best, it was only an indirect help which would occupy some of Napoleon's forces. What he needed was direct help, a few thousand men who were not yet battle weary, to stop the gaps in the line, or to join it on the left so that he could move some of his own men towards the centre. He had been sending aides all the afternoon along the ridge and beyond it to report on the Prussians' progress or to try to hurry them. Now he sent another, a colonel named Freemantle, to tell the nearest Prussian commander that the situation was desperate and to ask for help at once. Freemantle found the commander of the leading Prussian corps, General von Zieten. Von Zieten promised to come as soon as the whole of his corps was assembled, but he was reluctant to commit it to battle bit by bit—which was a sound enough conventional decision. Freemantle, fretting with respectful impatience, said he could not go back to the Duke with an answer like that. But von Zieten kept him waiting while he sent one of his own officers forward to reconnoitre. And that officer, like Ney's scouts, saw the crowds of wounded, deserters and prisoners making for the forest, and came back to report that Wellington was in full retreat. Freemantle could not contradict him; by then, so far as he knew, it might have happened. And von Zieten turned his troops and started to march away to the south, to support the rest of the Prussians at Plancenoit.

*　　*　　*

To every man on the crossroads at the centre of the allied line, isolated by the smoke, it was plain that the ultimate crisis had come, and that the next move in the lethal game was out of their hands. The Duke himself could do no more than he had done. Something, they knew, must come through the smoke from the sunlit world outside. Either another huge French column would come up the road ahead, and then the day would be lost—or else a Prussian column would come along the lane from the left, and then there might still be another chance. There was an outcry among the men to do something, not simply to wait while the musketry and grape-shot felled them all. Some shouted to the Duke—they wanted to make a last charge, to come to grips with the enemy and finish the thing for better or worse. He told them to wait, and hold on, and promised their chance would come. But he knew, and they all knew, that the French only had to hit them once more to win, and nobody doubted that the great Napoleon was preparing that final blow.

*　　*　　*

Ney also knew the moment for the final blow had come. He was certainly as near as La Haye Sainte, possibly nearer, and nobody there could have failed to know that the fire of Wellington's army was weakening round the crossroads. But he had nothing left to deliver the blow. The men he was using as skirmishers were the remnants of divisions defeated in the morning. His cuirassiers were makeshift units, survivors of all the regiments that had charged. All of them were as exhausted and shocked by battle as the British and the Germans. He had nothing left—but the Emperor had: fourteen regiments of the Garde Impérial had been in reserve near the Emperor's post at Rossomme all day, not even in cannon range. Ney sent a colonel galloping back to the Emperor to ask for a small

La Belle Alliance in 1815: Napoleon's second position was just behind the inn . . .

reinforcement of infantry. And the Emperor chose to receive the request with petulance. 'Troops?' he replied. 'Where do you expect me to get them? Do you expect me to make them?'

This was the supreme chance that Napoleon missed. At this moment, a last small effort, a few of the idle regiments of the Garde, could have broken the centre of Wellington's line and opened the road right through to Brussels. The effort had to be made at once —there was only an hour and a half to nightfall. He only had to say yes. But he would not do it. He did nothing.

The Emperor had roused himself from his mound at Rossomme. About three o'clock, according to Prince Jerome, he had retired to Le Caillou to treat his piles. Some time after that, he mounted and rode forward to another mound, close to La Belle Alliance. Earlier in the day, this move might have made a decisive difference. This

. . . and today

was the post of command he would surely have chosen if he had been in good health—a post corresponding to Wellington's, from which he could see the whole of the valley, observe events for himself and keep the battle under direct control. But now, the crossroad and the whole of the centre of the ridge was totally hidden by gunsmoke. He still was unable to see what Ney was doing, and Ney's colonel, by all accounts, was unable to make him listen. To send a mere colonel, indeed, was unlikely to make the Emperor think the matter was important: in the Grand Army, colonels visibly trembled when the Emperor was angry, and did not persist in what they had to say.

This was the immediate reason why he missed the chance: he simply did not know the chance was there, and nobody succeeded in telling him. And there was a further reason for his annoyance. He

did not know that Ney was on the verge of victory—but Ney did
not know that the rear of the army was now in peril. The fight
against the Prussians at Plancenoit was still undecided. The main road
back to France, the only line of communication, was threatened by
their advance: already, their cannon fire was falling not far short of
it. The Emperor could see what Ney could not—a danger that the
French might be surrounded. Possibly, it seemed, the whole of the
Garde might be needed to avert that danger.

But the basic cause of the Emperor's ignorance, and perhaps of his
irritability, was his illness—the illness which had kept him so long
out of sight and out of touch behind the lines. Few men can enter
the mind of a military genius, but illness reduces all men to a level;
and so perhaps it is possible and permissible to imagine the state of
Napoleon's mind at this moment, and to pity him in his dilemma.

'The Napoleon we knew does not exist any more': ever since
Ligny, his staff had been worried about him. But they did not understand he was in physical distress. Of the four men who knew—himself, his doctor, his brother and his valet—only he knew how far his
distress was affecting his judgement. By that time in the afternoon,
he must have known he was unfit to fight a battle as it should be
fought: he must have felt the whole thing was too much for him: he
must have longed, like any human, to lie down and rest until he felt
better. In secret, he must have acknowledged the appallingly bad
luck that a passing physical failure, on this day of all days, should
have sapped so much of his energy and skill. And he must have been
half aware by now of the awful, unthinkable possibility that his
weakness was going to lead him, before the sun went down, to an
utter irretrievable disaster.

In the solitude of his power there was nobody he could confide in,
nobody he could turn to for help or sympathy. Each question, each
request and each decision, can only have been an added harassment.
His sarcastic rejection of Ney's request suggests the self-pity and
exasperation of a man in authority who suddenly feels his burden is
intolerable and unfair: it was almost like a distracted parent's cry,
'Can't you see I'm busy?' He was possibly in a fever, and feverish
emotions may have influenced his mind. Ney, he believed, had
destroyed the cavalry. Had he been wrong to trust him? Now he
was asking for the Garde, the symbol of imperial splendour, the men
who were carrying parade dress in their knapsacks for the Emperor's

triumphal entry into Brussels. Command of the Garde had always been his own prerogative. Would Ney destroy them too? Or if he succeeded, would it be said that Ney had won the victory? It was impossible: Ney had gone too far, and asked too much.

* * *

While the Emperor hesitated, General Müffling was riding urgently along the British ridge. As Blücher's representative at Wellington's headquarters, he had a special anxiety about the progress of the Prussian army and felt responsible for the delays, and the hopes that had been deferred all the afternoon. And by now he knew, like everyone on the staff, that if his own people did not come in the next few minutes, the battle might be lost before the sun went down. When he reached the end of the line, above the farm of Papelotte, he saw, to his astonishment and horror, the troops of von Zieten marching away from the battle. He spurred his horse and galloped after them, down to the bottom of the valley.

From time to time all through the afternoon, the outcome of the battle had hung by the thinnest threads. Now for some minutes everything depended on this solitary Prussian, his horse and his powers of persuasion. He overtook the retreating troops, and by luck he soon found von Zieten. The appearance of a general all alone, on a sweating horse and in a state of desperate anxiety, made von Zieten halt. He was reluctant to countermand his order and turn his men round again. 'You are mistaken,' Müffling assured him, 'the British are not in retreat, they are standing fast. But the battle is lost unless you come back at once.' At last, von Zieten turned his men; and in doing so he turned the tide which had reached its lowest ebb. In fifteen minutes, his advance guards were in action at the end of Wellington's line. British cavalry which had been stationed there all day was moving along the back of the ridge to support the wavering centre. And the news was spreading along the line from man to man and from regiment to regiment: the Prussians had come.

* * *

Some of the French infantry saw them coming, and exhausted as they were the sight was too much for them. Their attack on the

Napoleon views the field from La Belle Alliance

crossroad began to slacken. Napoleon, on the mound at La Belle Alliance, saw them, still in formation, emerging from the smoke and beginning to return across the valley. And to hold them he sent a general of his staff along the line to spread the story that Marshal Grouchy and his army had arrived, and victory was certain.

Napoleon could not have believed this was true. He knew Grouchy could not have made the march so quickly, and he knew the Prussians were in strength on his flank, right across the route that Grouchy would have to take. Some of his staff had heard gunfire far away to the east, and assumed that Grouchy was in action somewhere. It is possible that Napoleon's order to the general was misunderstood: he may only have meant to announce that Grouchy was in action, not that he had reached the battlefield itself. But that excuse was never made for him. His order was accepted afterwards, even by his faithful supporters, as a deliberate deception, a ruse to arouse the morale of his men again. To play with an army's morale in such a way might have a momentary success, but was certain to have a reaction when the army found it had been told a lie. If it was deliberate, it was a desperate measure. But momentary success was what he needed, in the last of the daylight: the reaction, he may have thought, would be lost in victory.

For the moment, it did succeed. While the news of the Prussians' arrival was spreading through Wellington's army, the rumour of Grouchy's arrival spread through Napoleon's. Martin heard it somewhere on the slopes near La Haye Sainte: it put new heart into the remains of his division, and he heard fresh shouts of 'Vive l'Empereur!' go echoing up the valley. Captain Robinaux heard it outside the walls of Hougoumont—and he had also had a glimpse of Ney, not long before, and heard him shouting 'Courage! France is victorious! The enemy is beaten everywhere!' Young Silvain Larreguy heard it, down in the Hougoumont woods, and he and his friends felt their courage come back to them. Everyone in the rank and file believed it implicitly. Those who could see von Zieten's troops believed against all reason that they were Grouchy's. The Emperor's staff and the senior officers knew it was a lie, and Ney at least was angry at the deceit. But once the lie had been told, only a traitor could have told the truth.

*　　　*　　　*

It was half past seven. The sun was low behind the woods of Hougoumont, shining blood-red through the battle-smoke. There was another lull, except for the incessant cannon-fire. Both armies waited, sparring like prize-fighters in a final round, both too exhausted to make a decisive move. And in the lull, men who were sheltered from the shot looked round again and noticed things beyond the immediate need to kill and avoid being killed. William Leeke, the Ensign of the 52nd Foot, was half way between Hougoumont and the crossroads, stolidly standing in his place in the line and carrying the regimental standard: and what he noticed, suddenly, was the smell, a mixture of gunpowder and trampled crops.

His regiment had not had a chance for much active fighting, but it had withstood the cannon-fire all day. Now it had retreated forty yards behind the ridge, into the zone of comparative safety so many of the infantry had found. There was a low bank in front of him, the same bank that had sheltered Mercer's troop in the cavalry charges. The round-shot coming over it just missed the heads of the line of men behind it. Some which hit the bank bounded over them, and some almost spent rolled gently down the slope towards them. He saw one coming as innocently as a cricket ball, and put out his foot to stop it—but his sergeant, who had looked after him all day, told him in time that it still had the power to hurt.

It was a long time since Leeke had had to hide his tears that morning at seeing two dead men. Now he could see hundreds. All the buglers of the regiment had been sent to help the wounded to the rear, but nobody else had been allowed to go. Under the bank, a score of dying men were lying covered by their blankets. Two, still on their feet, were staggering back, each with his arm almost severed below the shoulder, each holding the mangled limb with his other hand: he thought they must both have been hit by the same shot. He stepped aside for a rifleman, led away with a terrible wound in his head. To his left, along the bank, were dead and wounded horses, the debris of the cavalry charges. Some, with their legs shot off, were still eating the trodden rye. And two yards in front of him, inexplicable, lying in the mud, was a dead tortoiseshell kitten.

The lull was broken by a single horseman. A French cavalry officer galloped up the ridge, through all the flying shot, with his sword in its sheath, shouting not '*Vive l'Empereur!*' but '*Vive le roi!*'

He rode up to Sir John Colborne, who commanded the 52nd. 'That scoundrel Napoleon is over there with the Garde,' he said, pointing towards La Belle Alliance. 'That's where the attack is coming from.' Colborne sent an officer to the Duke's headquarters with the warning. And a few minutes later, the Duke rode past in front of Leeke's position, all alone, with his telescope in his hand, still seeming as calm as ever.

The deserter's information was not much help to the Duke: he had already done all he could to strengthen the line, bringing in the last remnants of reserves from the flanks to the centre. But at least it warned the ranks of the 52nd, who could not see over the ridge. So they were not surprised when they heard the drum-beats coming, the rum-a-dum, the *pas de charge* of Napoleon's infantry, and the growing shouts of *Vive l'Empereur*.

*   *   *

Half an hour had passed since the Emperor had rejected Ney's request with sarcasm: now he had made up his mind to do exactly what Ney had asked. He had ordered forward five battalions of the Garde Impérial. And crying 'Let everyone follow me' he had put himself at the head of them and marched down the highroad into the bottom of the valley.

It was not a mere whim that had made him change his mind. In that half-hour, two battalions of the Garde had attacked at Plancenoit and turned the Prussians out of the village, and so removed the immediate threat to the flank and rear of his army. But in the same half-hour, Müffling had brought von Zieten back to the ridge and, with that reinforcement on his left, Wellington had moved his own units and plugged the worst of the gaps in the centre of his line. At seven o'clock, the Garde could have marched straight through. At half past, the issue was in the balance again.

Throughout the open slopes of the valley, French soldiers saw the solid phalanxes of the Garde approaching in the smoke, and none of them doubted that this was the Emperor's master-stroke. The men of the Garde were sometimes called the Immortals. The name had a double meaning. In their own eyes, it meant that the fame of their deeds was immortal. But among other more ordinary soldiers it had a jealous and sarcastic undertone, because the Emperor had so often

Napoleon's generals begged him not to expose himself to greater risk

seemed to keep them in safety and out of action until the moment when a battle was almost won. For both reasons, however, the solemn approach of the Garde was a sign that victory was near. And to those who were close enough to see the Emperor riding at their head, it seemed certain. Wounded men, as the columns passed them, raised their heads or struggled to their feet to cheer them. A veteran sitting by the roadside whose legs had both been crushed by a shell repeatedly shouted 'This is nothing, comrades. Forward! Long live the Emperor!'

Perhaps for a few minutes the Emperor had thought of leading

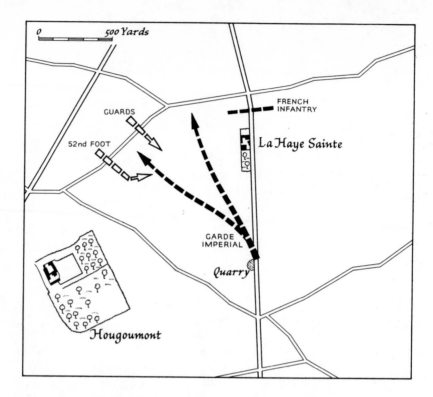

them into the battle itself. But he did not ride in front of them very far. At the bottom of the valley, on the left of the road, there was a quarry, and he turned into it with his staff and let the columns pass him. According to one of his aides-de-camp, the staff was divided in its opinion. Two of his attendant generals were begging him not to expose himself to any greater risk—the safety of France, they said, depended entirely on him. But Prince Jerome was heard to ask another general: 'Can it be possible he will not seek death here? He will never find a more glorious grave.' Jerome, it was clear, did not believe that France could still be saved. But he might have known that his brother would never admit he was beaten.

The old warriors of the Garde, the same observer thought, looked surprised and discontented to see the Emperor there when they had been told he was leading them. But they marched past with their customary firmness and precision. There was a savage silence in their ranks.

Beyond the quarry, Ney took command of them. The Garde as yet was unmarked by battle: Ney was sweating, muddy, dishevelled, and had lost his hat—his red hair made him more conspicuous without it—for he had fought and ridden harder all day than any other soldier. Ahead, the road led straight up the ridge to the crossroads where Wellington's troops were reduced to exhaustion. Right up to the last hundred yards, that road was in his hands. But he did not go that way. Just after the quarry, before the orchard of La Haye Sainte, he turned off to the left and marched up the open fields between La Haye Sainte and Hougoumont, where the cavalry had charged so many times and failed.

Nobody knows why he did so. Possibly, the road was too restricted for the movement he had in mind. Possibly, since he knew the Prussians were coming from his right, he believed that the opposition would be weaker on his left. Or possibly, tough as he was, he was too exhausted by then to make a calm decision. But that way, the Garde had to march a thousand yards exposed to artillery fire, through mud that the cavalry had churned to a liquid. And Wellington's men at the top, although they had been decimated by the cavalry, had had a couple of hours' comparative rest. Half way up, Ney's horse was killed by a cannon shot and he fell heavily. It was the fifth time that day. He disentangled himself and tramped on, beside the leading column, hindered by his heavy cavalry boots. And first round-shot, and then grape, began to tear holes in the mass of marching men.

Whatever Ney's reason for choosing to go that way, Wellington had foreseen the possibility. He had already ridden along that part of his line, redeploying the artillery and disposing the infantry in ranks four deep—a compromise formation which would give more fire-power than squares would give against oncoming infantry, and yet be strong enough in depth to resist whatever remnants of cavalry the French could bring with them. In that formation, most of the infantry remained lying down behind the crest. When everything was ready, he stationed himself on the spot where he expected the main attack, behind two battalions of the 1st Foot Guards commanded by a general named Maitland. Upwards of a thousand men, if they glanced behind them, could see him there, apparently unconcerned at the danger he had told them to avoid by lying down. And on horseback he could see beyond them, down the hill.

The French were coming in ranks of sixty men abreast, with intervals between their companies which made the whole column four or five hundred yards long. Passing Hougoumont, the battalions began to separate, by inclining to their left in echelon. To the Duke and other officers, that seemed to indicate a simultaneous attack in different places. But neat manœuvres in column were impossible in the mud and among the fallen men who were killed or wounded in the leading ranks by gunfire. Here and there, the column disappeared from the sight of the British officers, hidden by smoke and the undulations of the ground. And when it emerged on the final slope, it had coalesced again into two columns, one opposite the 1st Foot Guards and another, somewhat smaller, to the left. On the flanks of both there was light artillery, and to the rear, near Hougoumont, some units of cavalry; and all over the field, French infantry re-aroused by the Garde's example was advancing in support. As the range decreased, every British and allied gun that could be brought to bear was loaded with double charges of grape and wrought havoc in the close-packed columns. But still they came on, and on, carrying their muskets at the port, their officers out ahead of them waving their swords.

The major column, right up to the crest of the ridge, met no infantry and saw none ahead of it. The Duke, who could see it, let it come. The guardsmen lying on the ground in front of him saw nothing until the tall bearskin caps of the French came over the crest forty paces away. And hundreds of them at that moment heard his voice behind them: 'Now, Maitland! Now is your time!' And a few seconds later: 'Up guards! Make ready! Fire!'

'Up guards! Make ready!'

It was often the youngest men who retained the clearest impression of moments of crisis, perhaps because they watched with eyes that were fresh to battle scenes. A youthful ensign of the Guards remembered jumping to his feet, and remembered the volley of musketry his regiment poured at the advancing column: to him, the column seemed staggered by it and convulsed. Part of it halted and returned the fire, part tried to advance, and part seemed to be turning round. In less than a minute, 300 Frenchmen fell. Somebody shouted 'Now's the time, my boys,' and the Guards leaped forward with their bayonets, over the gruesome barrier of corpses.

Gronow the Etonian dandy, who was not much older, remembered the charge and the cheer that went with it: the Garde seemed to him to be paralysed by the sudden impetuous attack. He saw French veterans, soldiers of long experience, killed by sword and bayonet without any effort to fight back: a Welsh soldier he knew by sight, because he was six feet seven inches tall, slaughtered a dozen with his bayonet and the butt of his musket.

None of the front ranks of the column survived to tell their story. They had been taught to believe in their own invincibility: they did not expect determined opposition. But in what had looked like a gap in Wellington's line, four ranks of redcoats must have seemed to rise out of the ground in front of them, so close that before the column could be halted, the ranks behind had pressed them forward to their death.

To the left, for a moment, the lesser column won the psychological victory it expected. The 30th Foot, in which Tom Morris was a sergeant, had been standing in square on top of the ridge. When the light artillery of the French advanced into grape-shot range, the regiment was ordered to retire behind the crest. As it began to move, wounded men clung on to their friends for fear of being abandoned. Another battalion—it was never identified, but it was British—also retreated in a hurry, the two collided, and both were tangled together in a mob which was pushed along by the pressure of men behind it. Officers caught in the crush were cursing and shouting orders to halt or—one of them recollected—crying with shame and rage: soldiers laughed and struggled and shouted, 'By God, I'll halt, sir, but I'm off my legs.' And all this happened before the French column was in musket range: its appearance alone had caused the rout. The advancing officers of the Garde Impérial saw it without surprise.

But on the right, the 52nd Foot reacted in a totally different way, and William Leeke, still proudly carrying the regimental colour, was suddenly in the hottest of the fight. Sir John Colborne, who commanded the regiment, saw the column coming obliquely up the hill to his left and ordered an advance. And the regiment went over the ridge, not in a charge, but marching in line, preserving its orderly four-deep ranks. At the sight of the French columns, three or four hundred yards away, the 52nd answered the shouts of '*Vive l'Empereur*' with three cheers. When the left of the regiment was opposite the head of the main French column, it began to mark time, and the word of command 'Right shoulders forward' came down the line from Colborne, repeated by the mounted officers and company commanders: and the whole line, in a parade-ground movement, wheeled to the left until it faced the flank of the Garde Impérial.

Looking back up the hill, William Leeke had a momentary glimpse of the ridge from a Frenchman's point of view: it looked deserted, he could not see any British troops up there at all. But more in his mind as the clash approached was the thought of what would happen to his soul if he was killed. He quietened his fear by reflecting that all who believed in Jesus Christ would be saved, and since he did believe he would be all right. At the age of seventeen, he had every excuse to be afraid as he marched on, with his conspicuous standard, towards the mass of the enemy. But after his month in the officers' mess, nothing could have made him admit he was afraid. There, on either side of him, were the men who had teased him, advised him, drunk his brandy, treated him with a rough kind of fatherly affection, taught him regimental pride—and then had trusted him to carry the symbol of it. Some of these friends were ahead with the regiment's skirmishers, some mounted and riding in front of the ranks, and some like himself on foot among the soldiery. He saw one he had specially admired, a major named Chalmers: he had put his cap on the point of his sword and was standing in his stirrups and cheering the regiment on. And then the front ranks fired an opening volley, and half-halted to reload while the third and fourth ranks passed through them to fire in their turn.

At the volley, the French column halted and its left-hand files turned outwards to face the attack. This was the moment when the 1st Foot also opened fire on the head of the column; but blinded by smoke and blinkered by intense excitement, the two regiments for the most part were out of sight of each other, and each was to claim ever after that it had attacked alone. Leeke saw the flash and the smoke of the French muskets. He and the regiment marched on, closing the gap towards the point of a bayonet charge, in a duel of musketry at ever-shortening range. In a minute or two a score of the officers he knew were hit, and he witnessed the instant terrible transition from pride and energy to agony and bloody wreckage—one carried away by his horse, grasping the pommel of his saddle, blood pouring from his head, one hit in the temple, one without a leg, one shot through the lungs, one desperately wounded in the groin. And Leeke, barely conscious of anything but the duty he had been taught, marched on unarmed, for an ensign needed both hands to carry the colour and did not draw his sword.

The Garde Impérial did not wait for the bayonet charge. Attacked from ahead and from the flank by the fire of far more muskets than they could bring to bear, their formation crumbled away and they broke and ran. The Guards charged after them until they sighted cavalry, which made them return in some confusion to the ridge. The 52nd, still in line, continued its stolid march across the slope that had been in the hands of the French all day. They passed over the dead and wounded of the Garde, lying thick on the ground where the column had halted. Leeke had to jump over heaps of them lying on top of each other. He had a glimpse of Sir John Colborne on foot—his horse had been killed—wiping his mouth with a handkerchief. And suddenly in the smoke, an onrush of horsemen, at the gallop towards the line. The regiment fired, those who were still loaded, and some of the riders crashed down, but the line opened to let the rest pass through. They should have received the charge on their bayonets, Leeke thought, and he made for the gap and began to draw his sword to attack the leading horseman. The loop of the sword knot was entangled with the scabbard, and to his dismay the sword would not come out. He lowered the colour, intending to use it as a lance. But the horseman was shot and fell in front of him. And then he saw the stripes on the man's arms: he was an English sergeant. 'It's always the same,' a mounted officer was heard to say. 'We always lose more men by our own people than we do by the enemy.' And Leeke, ashamed of himself, and thankful to escape from the blunder, raised the colour again and kept it raised. The horsemen in

fact were a mixture of German, English and French: the 52nd was
not alone any more. The battle was on the move.

*   *   *

'The Garde is retreating': the news spread almost instantly among
the French from Hougoumont to Plancenoit: a French historian
wrote that it was the death-knell of the Grand Army. The morale of
the army, the frail mass-opinion that holds an army together and
makes it fight, broke suddenly and irretrievably. Shouts of 'We are
betrayed' were heard, and 'Sauve qui peut.' Betrayed by whom? By
their own officers, men insisted afterwards—the officers who had
told them Grouchy was there. Suddenly every man understood the
story was untrue. Some understood it had been a deliberate lie. Few
knew or could have brought themselves to believe that the Emperor
himself had told the lie. But all of them of every shade of loyalty
knew they were beaten.

Martin saw the Garde begin to run. Other men in front of him
turned with the stamp of panic on their faces, ready to fight their
way through their own ranks to get away. So he turned too and ran:
there was nothing else he could do, the thing was infectious and
inevitable. Sylvain Larreguy had been led up the ridge, close behind
the Garde, advancing blindly, doing what he was told; and when
his regiment stampeded, he had a glimpse of Ney, dismounted, bare-
headed and dirty, a broken sword in his hand, abandoned by his
aides-de-camp and servants. He was shouting to rally some men—
'Come and see a Marshal of France die'—and a handful of them
formed a rank under his command, but it was swept away. The
remnants of the entire army were converging in flight on the road
near La Belle Alliance—the road they had marched up in such glory
in the morning, the only road they knew that led back to France.

*   *   *

In the smoke and the gathering dusk, most of the British troops
could not see what was happening and did not know. An hour
before, defeat had seemed very near. Now even those who could see
could hardly believe they had won. The Duke rode back from his
place behind the Guards to the post by the crossroads where he had

started the battle. Ten minutes after the rout of the Garde began, he snapped his telescope shut, and took off his hat and waved it. Everyone who could see him understood. The English cavalry which had been recalled from the left of the line, still almost fresh to battle, charged over the ridge. The infantry cheered and marched forward. The advance spread out from the centre to the flanks until almost every man who could march was moving. The left of the crossroads was still so thick with smoke that Kincaid had seen nothing of the Garde's attack or retreat. The first thing he heard, through the battle din, was the cheering far over to the right, growing louder as it was taken up by one regiment after another. It made everyone prick up his ears, and the hard-pressed riflemen shouted hurrah in their turn and charged through the broken hedges of the lane and down the hill again with their bayonets. The Duke galloped up to them, and they cheered him too. 'No cheering, my lads,' he shouted characteristically, 'but forward and complete your victory.' The charge took them out of the smoke, and after so many hours shrouded within it, surrounded by desolation and fearful of disaster, Kincaid had a moment of delight and astonishment: a fine summer's evening, the French in panic flight.

The Duke rode on, beyond La Haye Sainte. His staff, those who were still in action, lost touch with him: somebody who went with a question found only one officer in attendance, who unexpectedly answered in French that he did not speak a word of English. He caught up with the 52nd and found them halted to dress their line: Ensign Leeke had been ordered out with the colour for them to form on. Sir John Colborne, having lost his horse, had just had the embarrassment of springing into the saddle of one which proved to be harnessed to an abandoned gun. And Leeke had been hit by a missile which he deduced, when he had time to think, had been the top of somebody's skull. 'Go on, Colborne, go on,' the Duke cried. 'They won't stand. Don't give them a chance to rally.' The regiment marched on again—and Leeke, in the van of it, believed for a minute or two that he was the foremost man in Wellington's army. They had almost reached the quarry where the Emperor had halted while the Garde marched past him. Straight in front of them on the road, some of the Garde who had not been in the forefront of the battle had re-formed in squares, and the Emperor—though the 52nd did not know it—had just taken refuge inside them. The 52nd was still

'He took off his hat and waved it. Everyone who could see him understood'

under heavy fire, from those few men whose discipline still held, and from isolated cannon, and from the Prussian artillery which was blazing away across the road from the east. Lord Uxbridge came galloping up and joined the Duke. 'For God's sake, Duke, don't expose yourself so,' he shouted—advice a good many people had wanted to give that day. 'I'll be satisfied when I see those fellows go,' the Duke answered, indicating the squares of the Garde. And a moment later Uxbridge was hit by a ball that had passed over the neck of Wellington's horse. 'By God, sir, I've lost my leg,' he is said to have cried. 'By God, sir, so you have,' the Duke replied. The knee was shattered; the Duke supported Uxbridge in the saddle until his aide-de-camp and some soldiers took him off his horse and carried him away.[1]

*   *   *

Mercer was left behind in the moment of triumph. While his battery was firing at the columns of the Garde it had come under fire itself, from artillery on high ground to the left, somewhere on the ridge beyond the crossroads. He had no time to wonder how a hostile battery had reached a position within the British lines: its shooting was rapid and appallingly accurate. His horses and limbers were below the ridge and had been protected from the front, but this flanking fire plunged in among them, knocking down the harnessed horses by pairs and making horrible confusion. His drivers were hardly extricating themselves from one dead horse before another fell, or perhaps themselves. He saw saddlebags torn from the horses' backs and their contents scattered: a shell exploded under the two finest horses in the troop and they both dropped dead. He turned his two left guns and began to shoot back, but so few of the gunners were still on their feet, and those few were so exhausted, that they could not run the guns up into position after they recoiled, and at each round they fell back closer to each other, and to the limbers. Mercer dismounted and served a gun himself, overcome by grief at the wreckage of the troop that had been his pride—and he saw a

[1] The source of these famous exclamations is unknown. It is not likely this is exactly what they said, if they said anything, but whoever invented the story succeeded in epitomizing their characters. Another even more evocative and even less likely version puts it the other way round: 'By God, sir, you've lost your leg.' 'By God, sir, so I have.'

black speck through the smoke, and instantly knew what it was and remembered you were never supposed to see a cannon ball coming unless it was going to hit you. He said 'Here it is then,' in a gasping voice as if cold water had taken away his breath—and 'whush' it went past his face, hit the point of his collar and killed a horse behind him.

A tall man in a black German uniform came galloping up to him. 'Mein Gott! Mein Gott!' he cried. 'Vot is it you doos, sair? Dat is your friends de Prooshians, und you kills dem! Vil you no stop, sair? Ah, mein Gott, vere is de Dook von Vellington?'

'Ride round the way you came,' Mercer said—and even then felt a flicker of amusement at the man's accent and consternation. 'Tell *them* they are killing their friends the English. The moment their fire ceases, so shall mine.'

At last the man rode away. But the remains of Mercer's troop was only saved by a Belgian battery, who seemed to him to be drunk, but were in a position to enfilade the Prussians and drive them off. In the respite, Mercer looked down the hill again, saw the valley covered by masses of troops that he could not distinguish from each other, heard a shout of 'Victory! Victory! They fly!'—and only then noticed that the cavalry and infantry had gone, and his battery was almost alone on the ridge among the dead and wounded. An aide-de-camp rode up, shouting 'Forward, sir! Forward!', and waving his hat like a huntsman laying on his dogs. 'How, sir?' Mercer asked: for 140 of his splendid horses were down, his guns and carriages were in a muddled heap, and even the men who were still untouched were blackened by smoke and covered by mud and blood, and were sitting utterly exhausted on the trails of the carriages, or lying on the wet polluted earth.

*   *   *

Like so many others all over the field, Captain Robinaux, down at the back of Hougoumont, could not see what was going on. The cannonade stopped, and the silence alarmed him. He waited for orders, but no word came from his senior officers. After a while, he went to reconnoitre, and walked for two or three hundred yards through the smoking woods. He was in time to see the whole of the army in full retreat.

Incredulous and horrified, he hastened back to his post, and ordered a retreat in column, but the panic soon struck his men. A few bullets came at them from behind, men looked over their shoulders, saw some cavalry and took them to be British. Some shouted 'We are lost,' men here and there broke rank and began to run, the column dissolved in disorder. And Robinaux ran after them, shouting 'Halt! Rally! Nobody is chasing us!'

To this simple man, who had spent the whole of his adult life contented under the discipline of the Emperor's army, it seemed as if heaven had fallen. He could not, and never did, believe the Emperor he adored had failed, or had deceived him. Possibly, he thought, the Emperor had mistaken the Prussian troops for Grouchy's, but Grouchy must have been there because the Emperor had said so: posterity would judge why Grouchy had not received the orders the Emperor had given him, and had not advanced at the proper time. Since the Prussians had attacked and Grouchy had not, the army was forced to retreat in face of overwhelming numbers. That was no disgrace. But there was no excuse for retreat to become a rout.

His shouts were useless. He ran for half an hour before he decided he must do something positive and drastic. Then he picked up a musket someone had thrown away, turned to face some dragoons who were overtaking him, shouted again that nobody was following, and promised to shoot the first of them who passed him. And by threats and determination, he managed to gather a dozen horsemen and, in the end, about sixty men on foot. He said he would lead them back to France; and he succeeded, because he still had the common sense to go across country, through the woods and fields, avoiding the road which he guessed would be choked by fugitives. His forlorn little troop marched all night and crossed the frontier in the morning—to begin a trek through northern France in search of someone who could tell them what to do.

*   *   *

Not many French soldiers were so lucky as to meet an officer like Robinaux: not many officers, seeing their men degenerate into rabble, made any more attempt to organize them. The army crammed itself into the narrow road, everyone pushing and fighting his neighbours to clear a way for himself. Men threw away their weapons and equipment, drivers of wagons cut their horses' traces, they stumbled over corpses, broken ammunition chests and abandoned cannons. The wounded, limping along too slowly for the rest, were thrust aside. Men who fell were trampled to death. And the deepening darkness added to the horror of the scene.

Conspicuous exceptions in the panic were the battalions of the Garde which had not been thrown into battle and were still on the road near La Belle Alliance. In them, the decades of training and martial pride held firm. While the mob streamed past them, a mixture of pursuers and pursued, they stood in square, retreating in orderly formation, and halting very often to repel attacks and close the gaps in their ranks where men had fallen. By their tenacity they may have saved the Emperor's life—he sheltered inside a square for a while—but they did not save their own. Under ceaseless fire, attacked by infantry and cavalry, the squares grew smaller until at last, somewhere beyond Rossomme, the remnants dissolved and vanished in the surrounding stream.

This show of discipline served no military purpose—things had gone too far for that. But when everything else was lost, it did preserve for the army a few last shreds of dignity and pride. It gave to men like Robinaux—and he was a characteristic Frenchman—something to admire, a noble story to tell. In the telling, the story grew to a legend, in which General Cambronne of the Garde, at the last extremity, cried 'The Garde knows how to die, but not how to surrender.' Cambronne, who was captured and survived, always denied he said anything of the kind: and another version was that when he was called on to surrender, he answered 'Merde'—a word that was vulgar but expressive and soldierly. But people continued to believe in the romantic exclamation—those words, as Robinaux described them, so worthy of the character and the beautiful name of France. In years to come, it was the kind of thing that many Frenchmen desperately needed to believe.

*   *   *

Mercer's clash with the Prussians was not the only one: Prussian and British cavalry charged each other, and all over the field there were isolated fights between the allies. It was not surprising, and nobody was to blame. The Prussians arrived without knowing the

The Emperor took refuge inside a square of the Garde

'Le Garde meurt et ne se rend pas!'

lie of the land, on a field of battle shrouded by smoke and fought
over all day by men of four nationalities in scores of different uniforms. A large part of Wellington's army spoke French as its native
language, and when British and Prussians spoke to each other, French
was often the only language they had in common. To both sides,
anyone with a foreign accent and an unfamiliar uniform looked like
an enemy, and it was safest to shoot first and ask afterwards.

Where there was no confusion, the meeting of the two armies was
cordial: a Prussian officer seized Leeke's colour in both hands and
pressed it to his bosom, exclaiming—in French—'*Braves Anglais.*'
But in the night mistakes would certainly have led to chaos and
disaster if both the armies had pursued the French. For that good
reason, the Duke decided to halt his army and leave the pursuit to
the Prussians.

Another good reason was that his army was exhausted. It had
fought for nine hours. A few of the Prussians, at Plancenoit, had
been in action for four hours, but von Zieten's corps had not been
in it much longer than an hour, and more units were constantly
arriving too late to take part at all.

It was more than mere physical exhaustion, it was nervous
exhaustion too. Wellington's men had expected death from second
to second all day, and for the last few hours most of them, in their
heart of hearts, had expected defeat. The experience left them unfit
to exploit their victory. They had won the day, and that was the
whole of a soldier's duty. The French had been brave and admirable
enemies, and they knew they were beaten: let them go. After the
carnage, every man was astonished and thankful to find himself still
alive, and he wanted to stay alive to enjoy the glory—the companionship, the boastful or affectedly modest stories, the free drinks from
circles of admiring civilians, the praise of pretty girls. In the back of
the mind of every man that night, whatever he had done all day, was
the knowledge that he had fought in the battle that had beaten
Bonaparte, and would have a hero's story to tell for the rest of
his life.

'This was the last, the greatest, and the most uncomfortable heap
of glory that I ever had a hand in,' wrote Kincaid. When the bugles
sounded the cease fire, he and the Rifles were somewhere near
Rossomme. Few people had got so far. Tom Morris's regiment was
so reduced it was unfit to fight, or even defend itself, and after a

token advance it bivouacked within fifty yards of the top of the ridge where it had fought all day. It had started the day with 29 officers and 550 men: at the end, 2 officers and 70 men were on their feet. During the attack by the Garde, there had been no officer left to carry the regimental colour, which was riddled with shot and almost falling off its staff: so they had wrapped it round the body of a trusty sergeant and sent him back to Brussels to keep the symbol safe. But Morris's only hurt was the cut on his face, and he still had some of the extra gin he had drawn in the morning. The drinking companion who had told him to save it gave him a slap on the back: 'Out with the grog, Tom. Did I not tell you there was no shot made for you or me?'

Sergeant Wheeler's regiment, in comparison, had suffered very little, and he had had the luck to spend the whole of the day in the shelter of the sunken lane. But when the advance came, all they did was follow some Prussian cavalry as far as Hougoumont. They halted in the orchard which was full of dead and wounded. Wheeler had the strong stomach of an old campaigner. He went and looked into the farmyard, where men of the Guards lay in heaps; many, he remarked, who had been wounded inside the buildings were roasted, and some who had tried to crawl out from the fires lay dead with their legs burnt to a cinder. He cooked himself some supper, wrapped himself in his blanket and slept very comfortably until daylight.

Private Clay, who had fought at Hougoumont all day, was more squeamish. He took out the piece of a pig's head he had tried to eat in the morning and started to roast it again on a clear flame in the burning building. But when he found that the fuel of the flame was a corpse, he lost his appetite, and could only eat some porridge he found, full of dust, in an abandoned pot, and some unripe fruit from the garden.

As another old hand, Sergeant Lawrence's first thought at the end of the battle was also of food. Nobody in his company had anything left to cook, but they foraged in the hundreds of wagons and thousands of knapsacks the French had abandoned, and his find was two fowls and a large ham, hidden in a sack of corn. He and two other sergeants boiled and ate the whole lot.

Even Ensign Leeke began to think of eating. The 52nd reached Rossomme, where the Emperor had spent most of the day, and they bivouacked on the straw the Garde Impérial had used the night before. Near by were the knapsacks of the Garde, lying in a square where they had been jettisoned, and Leeke's sergeant found a loaf of bread in one of them. 'Won't you have a slice, Mr. Leeke?' he said. 'I am sure you deserve it, sir.' Leeke was very glad of the bread, and he glowed at the compliment.

Gronow and the Guards finished the day in the orchard of La Belle Alliance. After a while, they heard the sound of trumpets, and he went to see what was happening. It was Blücher, arriving at the head of a Prussian cavalry regiment. And while Gronow watched—he had a courtier's genius for being on the spot on great occasions—the Duke came up the road from the opposite direction. The two commanders shook hands without dismounting: each of them greeted the other as victor. A Prussian band struck up 'God Save the King', and Prussian infantry sang the hymn 'Now thank we all our God'. 'Quelle affaire!' old Blücher exclaimed—the Duke said afterwards it was all the French he knew. Blücher agreed to manage the pursuit, and proposed that the battle should be called La Belle Alliance. But when Müffling repeated the suggestion later that evening, the Duke made no reply, and Müffling understood he had no intention of agreeing. Müffling thought he did not want to over-emphasize the part the alliance had played in the victory, and there may have been some truth in that. But it was a poor suggestion anyway. The Duke could hardly have been expected to give his victory a name that was purely French, or to call it after the inn the Emperor had used. It was lucky his own headquarters had a name that looked almost English.

After the meeting, Blücher rode on to Genappe where he stopped for the night and sat down, homely as ever, to write to his wife: 'My dear Wife, You remember what I promised you, and I have kept my word. Superiority of numbers forced me to give way on the 17th; but on the 18th, in conjunction with my friend Wellington, I put an end at once to Buonaparte's dancing. I had two horses killed under me yesterday.' And to somebody else he wrote that the strain had been too great for him, and he was trembling all over.

The Duke rode back from the meeting in moonlight across the battlefield, silent now except for the groans of the wounded and the rattle of musketry far away to the south. Between La Belle Alliance and La Haye Sainte he had to leave the road and pick a way beside it: it was completely blocked by abandoned French guns and wagons,

The two commanders greeted each other as victor

smashed and overturned. Only four or five of his staff were with him.
He seemed dejected, and did not speak to them. Crossing the fields
in the darkness, their horses shied and snorted, alarmed at the bodies
lying there unseen. In his quarters at Waterloo, the table had been
laid for the whole of the staff. He sat down at it alone, and people
noticed that whenever the door was opened he glanced at it eagerly,
as if he hoped to see some of his friends who had eaten breakfast
there and now were missing. When he had eaten, he lay down to
sleep on a pallet on the floor, because an officer was dying in his bed.

*   *   *

The rout of the French reached its ghastliest climax in the village of
Genappe, three miles beyond Rossomme. Between the houses of the
village, the road ran downhill to a bridge across the little river Dyle.
The bridge was only eight feet wide, just enough for a single wagon.
The army poured into the top of the street and was carried down the
hill by its own momentum: but it could only filter slowly out across
the bridge at the bottom. First the bridge and then the whole of the
street was blocked, and thousands upon thousands of men were

Genappe

crushed among the forage and baggage wagons which had halted
there in following the advance. In terror of what they imagined was
coming behind them, men tried to cut their way through, horsemen
slashed with their swords, infantry used their bayonets, shots were
fired. They killed and maimed each other without making any
progress: the living were only hampered by the dead. At the
entrance of the village, the rear of the rabble stood in a dense,
bewildered crowd, waiting its turn and unable to move a step: and
into this herd the Prussian cavalry rode with its lances and sabres.
Not until they were scattered by the charge did the fugitives think
of running round the village, avoiding the bridge and wading across
the stream, which was only nine feet wide and three feet deep. And
in truth there were very few Prussians in pursuit: their infantry had
halted, and perhaps 4,000 horsemen were pursuing 40,000 French.
But numbers had ceased to count. A drum-beat, a cheer, the sound
of a horse's hoofs was enough to drive the French to frenzy and start
the stampede afresh. The Prussians were said to have mounted a
drummer boy on one of Napoleon's carriage horses, and that boy
alone was enough to keep the enemy on the move.

The Emperor himself was in Genappe and saw it all: yet he was
still giving orders which nobody carried out, and making plans to
rally the army and save the day—unreal, ephemeral plans which he
abandoned one by one as events overtook them. He had left the
squares of the Garde to fight their gallant, futile action, and ridden
alongside the road with half a dozen officers of his staff and an escort
of a few horsemen, unnoticed in the mob. Even he took about an
hour to force his way down the street of Genappe. At the bottom of
the hill, before the bridge, he found his campaign carriage among
the jam of vehicles. He climbed into it and sat down. But before any
horses could be harnessed, he heard the cheers and shots of the
Prussians, and he got out again, hastily mounted his horse and
escaped across the bridge.

The carriage was captured a few minutes later, a symbol of pride
and downfall, pathetic in its intimate splendours. Among its equipment were a dinner service of gold, sanitary utensils of silver,
perfumery, a writing desk, pistols, a folding bed, and a *nécessaire*
containing nearly a hundred golden articles of toilet. There were all
the Emperor's medals, and his clothes: they included a spare uniform
which had diamonds to the value of 2,000,000 francs sewn into its

Symbol of pride and downfall

lining. And among his baggage were sheafs of printed copies of a proclamation addressed to the people of Belgium, and prematurely dated from the Imperial Palace of Laeken in Brussels:

'The short-lived success of my enemies detached you for a moment from my Empire: in my exile on a rock in the sea I heard your complaints. The God of battles has decided the fate of your beautiful provinces: Napoleon is among you. You are worthy to be Frenchmen. Rise in mass, join my invincible phalanxes to exterminate the remainder of those barbarians who are your enemies and mine: they fly with rage and despair in their hearts.

Napoleon.'

By midnight, these documents were blowing about the street of Genappe or lying neglected in the mud.

By that same hour, Martin reached Quatre Bras, three miles beyond Genappe. He was limping from the wound in his knee, and the broken foot a horse had trodden on in the charge twelve hours before. But he had avoided the slaughter of Genappe and was well in the lead, because he had fallen in with a young sergeant who knew the country well and guided him through it. On the field of Quatre Bras lay 4,000 corpses, all of them stark naked, for the Belgian peasants had stripped them of everything. It was like a gigantic morgue. The most hardened soldiers, passing through, were struck with horror there. The dead, alternately lighted by the moon and covered by the shadows of the clouds, seemed in some men's imagination to grimace and move their limbs.

A little way beyond that dreadful place, Martin found himself on the edge of a wood, and he saw a camp fire inside it, in a clearing. Hoping for company and warmth, he went towards it. Some men of the Garde were feeding it with sticks. And then he saw a man standing with his arms crossed on his chest, silent and alone among the trees, staring back along the road to Waterloo: the Emperor. He turned and crept away, moved and embarrassed by the glimpse of fallen majesty.

NIGHT

The wounded—The looters
The living—The dead

NIGHT

When darkness fell on the field of battle and the firing stopped, everyone found his ears were ringing and he was partly deaf from the hours of cannonade. For those who had not advanced, but had camped where they had fought, the deafness was a mercy. All of them could hear the groans and shrieks of the wounded close to them, but none of them could hear the sound of agony that must have gone up from the field as a whole, the two square miles where 40,000 men and 10,000 horses were lying helpless. How many were already dead, how many died in the night, how many had dragged themselves or been carried to barns or cottages—these figures nobody knows. But thousands and thousands, conscious and in pain, lay in the mud all night. While it was dark, nothing was done to help them, and a new insidious terror spread over the ridge and the valley. Even men who had fought and faced death all day, and were still unhurt, were afraid to move out of the circle of their bivouacs. It was partly a superstitious dread, and partly rational—for looters were busy, and although the battle was over, the killing was not.

*　　*　　*

Among the wounded, somewhere on the slopes below La Belle Alliance, was Colonel Ponsonby of the Scots Greys, the man who had last been seen that morning leading the cavalry charge against Napoleon's guns with both his arms hanging useless and the reins in his teeth.

His horse had carried him into the thick of the enemy cavalry, and he was cut down by a sabre and fell on the ground unconscious. When he came to his senses he raised his head to see if there was any escape—and a French lancer passing by saw the movement, shouted

'You're not dead yet,' and ran his lance through his back. Blood gushed into his mouth, his head fell again, he could hardly breathe and he thought he was dying. A French skirmisher stopped to plunder him, and threatened to finish him off. The colonel told him there were three dollars in his side pocket—it was all he had—and the man took them, but also tore open his waistcoat to look for more and left him lying in a painful position, unable to move at all.

Later in the day, while the battle still raged all round him, a kindly French officer gave him some brandy, turned him on his side and put his head on a knapsack—and told him he had heard that Wellington was dead and six British battalions had deserted. And some time in the afternoon, a cheerful French skirmisher used his body as cover, firing over him and chatting gaily while he loaded. 'You will be pleased to hear we are retreating,' he said at last. 'Good-bye, my friend.' And then, as the French receded, the Prussian cavalry rode over him at a full trot, kicking and lifting him off the ground and rolling him about most cruelly.

During the night, he found a man was lying on his legs, a man wounded like himself in the lungs: he could hear the breath wheezing through the wound. Prussians wandering about in search of plunder looked at him greedily, and one began to search him. He told the man he was a British officer and had been plundered already, but he would not stop and pulled him about roughly.

About midnight, an English soldier came by. Probably he was looking for plunder too, but when he found a wounded English colonel, he either took pity or saw a chance of reward. He heaved the dying soldier off Ponsonby's legs, picked up a sword and stood sentinel over him until dawn to protect him from other marauders. At six in the morning a cart came along, and Ponsonby was bundled into it and taken to Waterloo. He had lain on the field for eighteen hours with a punctured lung and six other wounds. The surgeons set to work to bleed him.

*   *   *

Looting the enemy's dead was a soldier's right, and fortunes were lying on the field for anyone cold-blooded enough to take them. Dead officers, in particular, had purses, watches, pistols, swords, lockets and sentimental charms. Their epaulettes and gold braid were worth money. When all those were gone, there were clothes and equipment, and when even the clothes were gone there were teeth. False teeth were either carved out of ivory or made up of human teeth, and dentists would pay well for the raw materials. Such a haul was made from the field of Waterloo that dentures for years afterwards were often called Waterloo teeth.

But the looting after Waterloo was out of hand. Wounded who resisted the looters were quietly stabbed, and successful looters killed and robbed each other. All the armies blamed the Belgian peasants for these excesses, but in the night after the battle few if any peasants had ventured back, and the prowlers were British or Prussian. The peasants' turn came later, when the armies had moved away.

*   *   *

Another British officer, who told his story but concealed his name, came round from unconsciousness after dark on the slopes of the

Colonel Ponsonby raised his head to see if there was any escape

ridge where the Garde had been defeated. He felt that heavy weights were lying on top of him, and he could not open his eyes. He moved his hand up to his face and found his eyes were sealed by clotted blood. He scraped it away and opened them, and saw a few inches from his own face the grinning mutilated face of a dead Frenchman who was lying on his chest. His legs were held down by the body of a horse. Near by, a young ensign was crying out for water. A Prussian soldier carrying a knapsack stopped to rob the ensign, who refused to give up some object he said was a present from his mother; and the officer saw the Prussian stab the young man to death.

The Prussian approached him next, and searched the soldier who was lying on top of him. But then he paused and listened, and threw himself down on the ground and pretended to be dead. Two other looters were coming, and they were speaking English. The officer called to them, and they heaved the horse and the Frenchman aside and gave him a drink. He was sure the Prussian would kill him if they went away, and he begged them to stay with him, or help him off the field. But they said they were sorry, they had to be back with their regiment before it was light. So he told them what had happened, and pointed out the Prussian shamming dead among the heaps of corpses. They said they would soon see to that: and they killed the Prussian and took his sack of booty.

*　　　*　　　*

Every man who lay wounded and yet survived the night told stories like these: the robberies and stabbings happened everywhere. But nobody did anything about it. Men who did not have the stomach for looting simply slept as best they could, close together for safety, while men all round them slowly bled to death.

The wounded were tormented by thirst. Every articulate cry was for water. But there was no water on the battlefield, except in the wells of the farmhouses and the stagnant ditches. Some wells were choked with bodies, and the ditches stank of blood and corruption, but nobody cared: if they could reach the water, they drank it. In cottages, they drank the water that had already been used for washing wounds.

The survivors were thirsty too. Before it was dark, Tom Morris had gone round among his wounded comrades, binding up some of their wounds and putting them in easier positions. All of them begged him for water, but he had none to give them—only gin, and he did not offer them that. When the night fell, he gave up trying to help and went to sleep like everybody else. He woke at midnight, with a thirst that he put down to the heat and exertion of the day, and the salt provisions: perhaps the amount of gin he had drunk had something to do with it too. So he set off to look for water for himself, picking his way among dead and sleeping men. But soon, the horror of the moonlit scene so terrified him that he ran back to where he had started, and woke his brother, who was in the same regiment, and asked him to keep him company. Together, it struck them they might find something to drink among the men of their own company who were sleeping soundly. They crept round, tapping on other men's canteens, and finally found a full one. Its owner was asleep with his head on it, but they unbuckled it, lifted his head without waking him, took out the full canteen and put an empty one in place of it. Then they sat down and drank it dry, and went to sleep again, and it never crossed their minds that the wounded all round them needed it more than they did.

*   *   *

Mercer also spent the night among the carnage, because he could not move the wreck of his battery. All the survivors of his troop lay down together a little distance away from the wreckage, which they said was too horrible to sleep with; but he made a kind of tent of a canvas cover on one of his limbers, and crept under that. His mind was too active for sleep. About midnight, he got up to contemplate the battlefield, now calm and still below the fitful moon.

Five paces away from him, a young French soldier was groaning: otherwise, deaf as he was, the scene of violence seemed to him to be quiet. Here and there, men were sitting up among the countless dead, trying to stop their own bleeding. From time to time, a man would struggle to his feet and stagger away a few steps to look for help, and fall again. Horses too would sometimes try to rise, or writhe convulsively. One in particular sat all night on its tail, looking about as if it expected help. It seemed to have lost both its back legs, and he knew it would be a mercy to shoot it, but after the bloodshed of the day he could not find the courage to do it, or even tell anyone else to do it: and when he moved away the following afternoon, the horse was still sitting there.

Looking up at the moon, Mercer thought of the homes it was shining on far away, and the people peacefully sleeping in them, not knowing yet that the men they loved were dead. From where he stood on the top of the ridge—so small was the battlefield—he could see the moonshine on unravaged woods and peaceful villages, and ripening untrodden corn. And all the horror and slaughter round him, he reflected, was to gratify the ambition of one man, who had risen from a station as humble as his own.

Mercer was a civilized, compassionate man, but while it was dark not even he thought of doing anything to help the wounded. He simply stood in his philosophic mood and watched them. When it was light again, he began to do a little, but by then it was too late for many of them.

The paralysis of the army in the dark seems strange in retrospect. Wellington, who rode back across the battlefield, and then sat down to his dinner and went to sleep, gave no order and made no suggestion about the wounded until the following evening. Nor did any other senior officer, so far as can be known. The army medical service was overwhelmed, and it was nobody else's business even to give first aid. Everyone was distressed by the groans and shrieks he could hear, but nobody walked a yard from his bivouac to fetch water or to help to bandage men who needed it. Everyone, of course, was tired, and that was some excuse. And the dark field, where friends and mortal enemies were lying mixed together, was genuinely terrifying. Above all, it was an unfamiliar situation, for which there were no standing orders. Battles seldom ended so suddenly, so conclusively, or so exactly at dusk: more often both armies had moved before nightfall, one in retreat and the other in pursuit, and both had to be ready to fight again the next morning. So active soldiers were accustomed to leaving their wounded companions behind with their dead and quickly forgetting them all. The idea of halting among them was unfamiliar, and nobody liked it. Some British regiments at Waterloo moved off the field before they bivouacked, simply in order to spend a quiet night. And the rest of them slept, compact little groups of healthy men among the sea of suffering, waiting like armies everywhere for somebody to tell them what to do.

*   *   *

As soon as daylight came, everyone was active again. Officers strolled about exchanging stories and asking for their friends: Kincaid observed that after most battles people asked who had been hit, but after this one they asked who was still alive. Thousands of people saw the spectacular end of two soldiers who tried to chop up a French ammunition cart for firewood: it blew up and threw them thirty feet in the air. William Leeke, who had innocently told his colonel a fortnight before that he thought he would wait for the first engagement before he bought a horse, now found he had not been foolish: he bought two for a few francs from a Prussian who had taken the trouble to round them up. He also bought a pair of brass-barrelled pistols, but that was a less successful bargain. He tried to use them to put a wounded horse out of its pain, but every time he pulled the trigger he missed, and he had to let a Prussian sergeant do the job for him. And then he saw his divisional general coming, and for fear of being asked where he had got the pistols, he threw them both over a hedge. While he was thus engaged, his regiment sent a fatigue party back across the valley to collect its own wounded and take them to the surgeons at Mont St. Jean or Waterloo. But not many regiments showed the same initiative.

Leeke, at Rossomme, had been spared the night on the battlefield: so had Gronow in the orchard of La Belle Alliance. But in the morning, when the Guards were marching away in belated pursuit of the French, they passed some carts full of wounded on the road, abandoned by their drivers. Some of them were Guardsmen, and one recognized Gronow and shouted 'For God's sake, Mr. Gronow, give us some water or we shall go mad.' He jumped into the cart and gave the man his flask, and the others begged him to fill it again from a ditch. He did so, and he also took off his cap, stopped up a bullet hole in the top of it with his handkerchief, and took them a drink in that. But this act of kindness was remarkable. 'I did not hesitate a moment,' Gronow himself wrote many years afterwards, as if he were still surprised at his own impulsive generosity: and clearly the rest of his regiment passed the cartloads of wounded men without doing anything.

During the morning, almost the whole of Wellington's army moved away to the south, and by late afternoon not a single healthy soldier was left on the field. Mercer's troop was the last to start, because it took him most of the day to replenish his ammunition,

The day after

repair his harness and round up enough ownerless horses to draw
four of his guns—and those four were all he could man. So he had
time to stroll about the field, and watch the beginning of the
aftermath of the battle.

At dawn, one of his sergeants had come to him for permission to
bury a driver named Crammond. 'And why Driver Crammond in
particular?' he asked. 'Because he looks so horrible,' the sergeant
said. 'Some of the men have not slept a wink all night for his eyes
looking at them.' The driver's head had been taken off by a cannon
ball, but his face was still attached to his neck; and that one exceptionally gruesome corpse, it seemed to Mercer, had taken the minds
of his men off all the other horrors. Crammond was immediately
buried, and immediately forgotten, and the troop went cheerfully
to work.

Of all the wounded, the French were most distressed, and Mercer
felt for them most strongly: as a soldier, he had no enmity for them
once the fight, and the night, were over. Left behind in an alien
country, they had no hope of rescue. He took water to those who
seemed to need it most, and with those who could speak he gossiped
about the battle: all of them, he found to his surprise, said their
officers had betrayed them. He tried to assure them all they would be
cared for, that the carts would be coming soon to take everyone,
friend or enemy, to the surgeons. This was true: when the work of
rescue began at last, there was not much distinction between the
sides that men had fought on. But they would not believe it. They
were sure they would either die by slow degrees or be killed by
Belgian peasants, and many of them begged him to kill them, saying
they wanted to die by a soldier's hand.

And with daylight, the peasants had indeed begun to congregate.
There were groups of them everywhere, men and women, busily
stripping the dead—and perhaps, Mercer thought, finishing those
who were not quite dead. Some were already staggering under
enormous loads of clothes, and some had collected firearms, swords
and bundles of medals and decorations. All were in high glee and
expressed unbounded hatred of the French—hatred they would
certainly have expressed of the British if the French had won.

Sightseers were gathering too. While Mercer and his men were
sitting down to dinner—their chairs were French cuirasses and their
food a muddy lump of veal that one of them found in a ditch—a

carriage drove down from the Brussels road and some smartly dressed gentlemen walked across the field. As they passed, they looked at Mercer and his filthy men with horror, but all pulled off their hats and made low bows. One in a high cocked hat approached the circle of men, holding a perfumed handkerchief to his nose and stepping delicately over the bodies so that he did not spoil his glossy silken hose. He made some polite conversation with Mercer about the events of the previous day, still using his handkerchief, and then took his leave, with many more bows, and picked his way towards Hougoumont, leaving a pungent scent behind him.

Hougoumont was the principal goal of the sightseers, not only the dandies from Brussels but officers and soldiers who had time to spare. Mercer was one who went to look at the place where the longest and fiercest battle had been fought. The courtyard was a sight more sickening and terrible than any he had seen: the fire had added a new dimension of horror. All the buildings were gutted except the chapel: the flames had charred the feet of a wooden figure of Christ on the cross, and there they had stopped. Even among the smouldering

Burial at La Haye Sainte

ruins, some men were still alive and were trying to bandage themselves, without any help from the peasants, the soldiers or the Brussels gentry. Mercer also left them. He ended the battle as he had begun it, in a garden. The garden of Hougoumont, which had been held successfully all day, still seemed untouched and tranquil within its high brick walls. A few dead guardsmen lay among the cabbages and turnips, but what were a few dead men? Birds sang and insects hummed among the flowers, the grassy walks smelled sweet. He did not want to leave it, or go back to work again.

*   *   *

During the day, the huge and horrible task of tidying up began. Most of the army's own wagons, and most of its doctors, had had to follow it in the advance towards Paris. So country carts were

Hougoumont: all the buildings were gutted except the chapel; the feet of the figure of Christ were charred

requisitioned to take away the wounded, local peasants were forced unwillingly to bury the human dead and burn the horses, and Belgian civilian doctors were pressed into service. Every cottage and farm at Mont St. Jean and Waterloo was already crammed with wounded men, and those who were still on the field had to be carted all the way to Brussels, whatever their condition. If they thought they were able to walk, they preferred to try, rather than endure the lurching and jolting of the unsprung wagons on the rutted, cobbled road. The road was jammed, the single journey took hours, the task as a whole took days. It was Thursday, four days after the battle, before the last men still alive were found and moved from the places where they had fallen. On the same day, at Quatre Bras where the rye was less trampled, men who had been hidden six days in it were still crawling out, deranged in their minds by hunger, pain and solitude.

Even when they reached Brussels, not much could be done for

them. The citizens, now relieved of any danger of backing the wrong side, were kind and solicitous. Rich men's houses were opened for the wounded, and ladies of quality busied themselves with making bandages, taking round refreshments, offering words of comfort and even dressing wounds. Some sent their carriages to Waterloo to fetch the wounded. The grisly work of amputation and bleeding went on, but the hospitals were full, and men were left lying in rows on straw in the streets. It was a matter of chance if a soldier was given any treatment, or lived or died without it.

Lord Uxbridge's was the most celebrated of the thousands of legs sawn off at Waterloo, and his attitude to the loss of it was typical. 'By God, sir, I've lost my leg' was a figure of speech, if he said it at all: the leg was not shot off, but the knee was shattered. After he had been carried to Waterloo in a blanket, three miles from where he was wounded, he discussed the chances of saving it with the surgeons. All agreed it would have to come off. While they were making ready, he wrote a letter to his wife and chatted with his staff about the victory. During the operation, he never moved or complained: nobody held his hands, although that was a common practice. He said once perfectly calmly that he thought the instrument was not very sharp—and indeed, by that time of day the surgeons were in

French wounded return to Paris

difficulties with knives and saws which were blunted by use. When it was over, his nerves did not seem shaken, and his pulse was unchanged. 'I have had a pretty long run,' he said. 'I have been a beau these forty-seven years, and it would not be fair to cut the young men out any longer.' Soon afterwards, another cavalry general came to see him. 'Take a look at that leg,' Lord Uxbridge said, 'and tell me what you think of it. Some time hence, I may be inclined to imagine it might have been saved, and I should like your opinion.' The visitor looked at the gruesome object, which was still in the same room, and confirmed that it was better off; and satisfied with that, Lord Uxbridge composed himself for sleep. Within a week, he was dressed and sitting up in a chair as if nothing had happened. Within three weeks, he was back in London, where a crowd took the horses from his carriage on Westminster Bridge and drew it through the streets, and the Prince Regent made him a marquess.

The owner of the house where the operation was performed, a M. Paris, shrewdly saw the value of the relic. He made a coffin for it, and with the permission of its owner he buried it in his garden. Above it he planted a weeping willow tree and put up a tombstone: '*Ci est enterré la jambe de l'illustre, brave et vaillant Comte Uxbridge . . .*'. Generations of people went to see the grave, to the benefit of the

Paris family, and Lord Uxbridge himself went back there some years later, and insisted on dining at the table he had been carved on.

*   *   *

The women were more in need of pity than the wounded. Officers, for the most part, who had their wives or lovers with them in Belgium, had left them in their billets or sent them to safety in Brussels or Antwerp. But private soldiers, with less money and possibly less sense, kept their wives with them on the march and in the bivouacs. A good many of these women had been there all through the battle, anxiously hovering on the edges of it. Some, hearing their husbands had been hurt, had dashed on to the field to try to help them and been wounded or killed themselves. Sad stories were told of corpses of married couples found lying together. But most, of course, failed to find their men, and had no way of knowing whether they were still lying there or had been carted away to Brussels; and these distraught creatures could be seen, when dawn broke again, hunting among the corpses and begging for news from any of the wounded who could speak.

The British believed that Frenchwomen often fought alongside their husbands in the army. It can hardly have been common, but one beautiful girl was found dead, in a French cavalry officer's uniform, on the ridge just below the crossroads, and to get to that place she must have charged with the cavalry. Of stories with a happy ending, the most notable was that of Mrs. Deacon. Her husband was a lieutenant, and she and their three small children had been with him before the battle started at Quatre Bras. In the evening, she heard he had been wounded, and she spent the whole of the night looking for him. On the next morning, Saturday, somebody told her he had been taken to Brussels, and she set off to walk there with the children. That day, the four of them walked all through the retreat from Quatre Bras. They crossed the field of Waterloo where the armies were assembling, and walked all night through the chaos of the Brussels road and through the rain, from which she was only protected by a shawl. On Sunday night, she found her husband, who had nothing worse than a shot in the arm, and on Monday she gave birth to a healthy girl, who was christened Waterloo.

But most of the wives and lovers, mothers and sisters of the combatants were far away, in Britain, France, Germany, Holland or Belgium, and they had to wait in anxiety, after the day of Waterloo, as they always wait after such manly follies. The news of the battle spread as fast as mounted men and semaphores and sailing ships could carry it. But the lists of casualties followed much more slowly, and even in the victorious countries, rejoicing was muted by fear of the cost of the victory. Ensign Leeke heard afterwards how his sisters had hidden the news of the triumph from his mother, who was ill, until the newspapers published the list of dead and wounded officers. Then they scanned through it, found his regiment, looked down the ranks and saw the entry Ensign William—and had a moment of anguish before they saw that it was not William Leeke but his fellow-ensign, another William, who was dead.

Such moments when the heart seemed to stop must have passed in hundreds of thousands of homes, to be followed by relief or misery. The awful dread was suffered by young Magdalene De Lancey who, three days before, had been so consciously happy, and then had waited in Antwerp so naïvely, trying not to listen to the rumble of the guns and hoping for a message from Sir William. And what happened to her epitomized this aspect of the battle—of any battle: the aspect that the heroes, in the excitement of the day, are able to forget.

The first casualty list, showing only senior officers, reached Antwerp the morning after the battle. An officer came to tell Lady De Lancey that a final victory had been won, and that her husband was safe: he had seen the list and Sir William's name was not on it. She rejoiced. But later in the morning, she was summoned by one of the senior ladies who had attached themselves to Wellington's headquarters. Everyone present looked so sad that Lady De Lancey felt she had to apologize for feeling happy. Then it came out—that the lady had copied the list, and in the hope of breaking the news more gently had left out Sir William's name: he was desperately wounded.

Cast down again from her happiness into intense anxiety, she made up her mind to go to Brussels to find him. While a carriage and horses were found, she tormented herself with the thought that each minute, as it passed, might make her a minute too late to see him alive. And on the road, it was no easier to be patient: her carriage was caught in a crowd of carts and horses, wounded men, deserters and refugees. She drew down the blinds to be alone. Half way to Brussels, a man she knew stopped the carriage.

'Do you know anything?' she called to him.

'I fear I have bad news for you,' he said.

'Tell me at once. Is he dead?'

'It is all over.' He had heard how Sir William had been hit and fallen in the Duke's company, and had seen the Duke's dispatch which reported him killed.

They took her back to Antwerp, and she shut herself in her room at the inn. In her grief that night, she thought that if she had only seen him alive for five minutes she would never have repined. Early in the morning, someone knocked at her door, but she did not want to listen to condolences and would not open it. But then, yet another informant sent her maid with a message: someone had seen her husband the day before, he was alive and asking to see her. The surgeons had bled him twice and even had some hope of his recovery. At first she refused to believe it: to hope, and then to lose hope again, seemed more than she could bear. But she was persuaded, and started her journey once more, in the same jam of traffic and the same desperate impatience. She passed through Brussels, and down the dreadful road to Waterloo—the carriage horses screamed at the stink of corruption—and in a cottage at Mont St. Jean she found him.

There in the hovel on the edge of the battlefield, they spent a third week of their interrupted marriage. They were alone, except for the peasants who had come back to their homes, and the surgeons who came to see them from time to time. He asked her at the beginning if she was a good nurse. 'I have not been much tried,' she said. He said he would be a good patient until he was convalescent, and then he knew he would grow very cross. She watched for a cross word, but in vain.

Before long, she knew he was going to die, and she must value every hour. But he did not know: he sometimes said the wound was a blessing, because he would never fight again and they could live a peaceful life, at home together in Scotland. She hid her despair, and never left him, and for six nights she hardly slept. The surgeons repeatedly bled him. She applied the leeches and blisters they ordered, washed him and brushed his hair, tore up the petticoat she was wearing to make compresses, contrived to find food and blankets, and sat beside him day after day and night after night, holding his hand and trying to talk to him happily whenever he seemed to want to talk to her. When at last the surgeons confessed they had no hope, she thought it was her duty to tell him. He said his only regret was in leaving her. That night, he said he wished she could lie down beside him, and she climbed into the back of the narrow wooden bunk he lay in, and for the first time since the battle a week before, both of them slept in peace. The next afternoon, she held him while he died.

Mont St. Jean was deserted by then, the humble primitive hamlet it had been before. The army had gone, far on its triumphal march to Paris, the glory was past, the bloody field was silent.

ILLUSTRATIONS

Half-title illustrations:
DAWN from scenes of army life by Swebach. British Museum, London.

MORNING, NOON, AFTERNOON and EVENING from George Jones's *Battle of Waterloo*, 1817. British Museum, London.

NIGHT from George Cruikshank's *Historical Account of the Battle of Waterloo*, 1817. British Museum, London.

PHOTOGRAPHIC CREDITS
John Freeman: pages 10, 13, 19, 22, 27, 37, 39, 40, 41, 45, 114, 117, 166, 175, 178, 192, 196, 212, 215, 216, 223.
Bibliothèque Nationale photographs supplied by R. B. Fleming

MAP CREDITS
The maps were drawn by Maureen Verity.

INDEX

Army, French, reviewed by Emperor, 44–50; routed, 182, 187; in retreat, 198–201 (*see also* Cavalry, French *and* Infantry, French)

Army, Prussian, 6; at Ligny, 36; at Wavre, 37; advance to support Wellington, 108–9; not yet arrived on battlefield, 125; think British are in retreat, 127; marching away from ridge, 164; at Plancenoit, 174

Army, Wellington's, 6; composition of, 7; Wellington on, 8; at Quatre Bras, 18; Wellington's opinion of, 26; relationship between officers and men, 26–7; moves away to south, 211

Cavalry regiments

Blues (Royal Horse Guards, *see also* Household Brigade), and the retreat from Ligny, 20; advances too far, 102

Cumberland Hussars, 143–4

Household Brigade (*see also* Blues *and* Life Guards), 131; charge by La Haye Sainte,

99–102; form into single line, 161

Inniskillings (6th Dragoons), 82

Life Guards (*see also* Household Brigade), and the retreat from Ligny, 20; in hand-to-hand fighting with French cavalry, 131

Royals (1st Dragoons), 82

Scots Greys (2nd Royal North British Dragoons), 102n.; behind the ridge, 82; charge the French, 94–6; advance too far, 102

Infantry Regiments

Black Watch (The Royal Highland Regiment, 42nd Foot), 82

Cameron Highlanders (79th Foot), 82

Coldstream Guards (2nd Foot Guards), 73

1st Foot (The Royal Regiment, later Royal Scots), 180

1st Foot Guards (Grenadier Guards), 178; Wellington and, 177; open fire on Garde Impérial, 180

231